. . . strongly favouring increased acc
this book has a warm style featuring ,..., ,
their experiences and feelings. Written expressly for teens, it would also be of
interest to parents, social workers and other concerned individuals.
– Transition

. . . based on conversations with forty adopted young people and includes their thoughts on a wide range of issues . . . can be very reassuring to teens, helping them know their own experiences are not unique; for parents and professionals it offers insights into feelings and concerns of teenaged adoptees.
– Adoptalk

Each chapter focuses on a particular topic of special interest to an adopted teenager. Recommended. – Library Materials Guide

. . . a valuable addition to the subject . . . a book written for adopted teenagers filled with a variety of different perceptions about environment, heredity, parents' need to adopt, feelings for parents, searching for beginnings, legal status and working with social workers. – CHQM radio, Vancouver

"We need to know what teenagers are thinking. This book should be required reading for every social worker." – Joyce Masselink, Social Worker, Consultant on Adoptions, Ministry of Human Resources, Family and Children's Services, Victoria, B.C.

"Books about adoption fall into several categories: How to adopt, parenting issues, children's stories, academic studies, searching for birth parents, and personal stories about adoptive families. Very little has been written for adolescence and almost nothing by them. Marion Crook has given adopted teenagers a voice and what they have to say should be heard by everyone involved, whether parents or professionals, and especially by every teen. This book clearly tells what its like to be a teenager adoptee." – C. Anne Lea, Chairperson, Adoption Council of Canada.

Books by Marion Crook

Non-fiction
Teenagers Talk About Suicide
Teenagers Talk About Adoption: The Face in the Mirror
NC Press Limited
Every Parent's Guide to understanding Teenagers and Suicide
International Self Counsel Press

Fiction
Stone Dead
Hidden Gold Mystery
No Safe Place
Cross Currents
Overlea House, Grolier, Inc.

Co-authored
How to Self-Publish and Make Money
Crook & Wise, Publishers

Teenagers Talk About ADOPTION

Revised Edition

MARION CROOK

NC Press Limited
Toronto, 1990

Canadian Cataloguing in Publication Data

Crook, Marion, 1941-
　　Teenagers talk about adoption

Rev. ed.
Previous ed. published under title: The Face in the mirror: teenagers talk about adoption.
Bibliography: p
ISBN 1-55021-047-5

1. Children, Adopted - Canada - Interviews.
2. Adoption - Psychological aspects.　I. Title.
II. Title: The face in the mirror

HV875.58.C3C76　1990　　　362.7'34　　　C89-093938-1

We would like to thank the Ontario Arts Council and the Canada Council for their assistance in the production of this book.

New Canada Publications, a division of NC Press Limited, Box 452, Station A, Toronto, Ontario, Canada, M5W 1E6.

Distributed in the United States of America by Seven Hills Distributors, 49 Central Avenue, Cincinnati, OH, 45202

Printed and bound in Canada

Cover Design: Don Fernley

To all the teenagers who opened their lives to me, and to my own children who add breadth and depth to my life.

CONTENTS

ACKNOWLEDGEMENTS

My thanks go first to the forty young people who gave me their time and their information. I agreed not to publish their names and so cannot thank them individually. Following is a list of people who gave me their time in interviews. We sometimes agreed, sometimes argued. Some are quoted in the book, some are not. All added greatly to my knowledge and I appreciated their interest and their caring attitude toward the teenagers I was trying to understand: **Mary Beauchamp,** Program Officer, Department of Social Services, Government of the North West Territories, Child Welfare League of America, New York; **Bill Crook,** law researcher; **Susan Drysdale,** Coordinator, Children in Care, Department of Social Services, Halifax, Nova Scotia; **Peter Hudson,** Department of Social Work, University of Manitoba; **Pam Hendy,** Canadian Adoptee Reform Association, Williams Lake, B.C.; **Anne Lea,** Adoption Resource Centre, Edmonton, Alberta; **Delores Lindsay,** mother of five, sociologist, Winnipeg, Manitoba; **Clair Marcus,** author, adoptee reform activist; **Joyce Masselink,** Social Worker, Consultant on Adoption, Ministry of human Resources, Victoria, B.C.; **Linda MacDonald,** President, Canadian Adoptee Reform Association, Richmond, B.C.; **Gwen McPherson,** mother, Victoria, B.C.; **Nancy Nelson,** Community Worker, Vancouver, B.C.; **Patricia O'Brian,** Acting Operational Support Coordinator, Ministry of Community and Social Service, Toronto, Ontario; **Irene Patterson,** Program Consultant for Adoption Exchanges, Fredericton, New Brunswick; **Rolland Perrin,** Psychiatric Social Worker, Department of Health, Williams Lake, B.C.; **Wanda Pillon,** Parent Finders, Victoria, B.C.; **David Ross,** Executive Director, Indian Friendship Centre, Williams Lake, B.C.; **Audrey Scrammell,** Director and Secretary, Canadian Adoption Reunion Registry, Victoria, B.C.; **Mark Spence-Vinge,** Supervisor, Department of human Resources, Williams Lake, B.C.; **Betty Stinson,** Social Worker, Department of Health and Human Resources, Whitehorse, Yukon; three birth mothers, **Anna K., Kelli A.,** and **Tammi K.** who gave me hours of their time. I am also grateful to the many parents and adopted adults who phoned me to tell me their story in the hope that it would help others.

FOREWORD

Imagine human life as a gigantic tapestry; pretend you are weaving your own life into that fabric, your ideas, your feelings and plans, slipping around and through the plans and ideas of others, weaving a circle into your family pattern that is expanded and complicated by the blending of new threads from many sources.

This book was written for you adopted teenagers who, like all teenagers, are entwined in your families' patterns and in the larger fabric of the world around you. You have something different from your friends, an extra trailing thread that may need attention before you feel complete. Some of you tie this loose connection to yourself and ignore it. Others trace it to its origin and leave it there. Others carry it as a burden that entangles all the relationships of their lives.

I read books to my children about adoption but, by the time they were twelve, I couldn't find any books in my city library or book store that spoke to teenagers. My two sons, both adopted as infants, never asked me about their backgrounds and I wondered what they were thinking. They answered my questions about it with brief "yes's" and "no's," and a kind of indifference. Didn't they care? Did any teenager care? Did anyone know what teenagers thought about adoption? My curiosity grew until I decided that I would find adopted teenagers and ask them, "What do you think about being adopted. What do you know? How do you feel?"

I borrowed every book I could in my local library. I used a friend's computer and did a search on all books in print on teenagers and adoption. I used another friend's university card and raided the college library. I read every book I could get my hands on that had anything to do with the subject.

Then in the summer of 1985 I packed my Dodge van, bribed my twelve-year-old son David to come with me and headed south. My friend Nancy, seven months pregnant, her eighteen-month-old son Max and Felicity, the twelve-year-old daughter of a Winnipeg friend, joined us in Vancouver. From there the caravan went east, gypsy-like, along the Trans Canada Highway–Max's playpen strapped to the roof rack. We stayed with friends and relatives along the way and I interviewed adopted teenagers who were daughters, cousins or friends of my friends. In this casual and random fashion we wandered over the prairies and arrived in Winnipeg where Delores, a busy mother of five with no time to look for adopted teenagers to interview, had put an ad in two city newspapers asking interested teens to call her number.

The phone rang for days. I crouched in the pantry (the only quiet room) writing down your names, ages, addresses and detailed directions to your houses. For four days I drove around the city listening, taping, asking you questions.

In the fall, I stayed in Vancouver, put an ad in a city paper and collected names and addresses that kept me interviewing for six weeks. I also did some interviews with friends' children, and friends of friends' children in my home town of Williams Lake, B.C.

The sample wasn't scientific. I couldn't control how many of you were eighteen, or how many were girls or boys; so I can't say that all the conclusions in my interviews are an accurate and typical reflection of the whole population of teenagers. I tried to get as varied a response as I could but I only interviewed forty of you and I certainly wasn't rigid about my criteria. I didn't do any interviews with kids who were not adopted so I don't know how they feel about these questions. I didn't look for statistics on whether adopted kids are more or less emotionally stable than their friends. I didn't see why you should be. For eighteen years I'd worked as a public health nurse and had a lot of contact with children and teenagers. I'd never seen any evidence that the behavior of adopted teenagers was better or worse.

I was afraid, when I started the interviews, that I wouldn't find out anything at all. My own two boys had lulled me into thinking that the circumstances of their birth were of academic interest only. In fact my oldest son, eighteen at the time, asked, "What are you doing a book on adoption for? Nobody cares." You surprised him and you surprised me. I suspected that there was some dissatisfaction but I truly wasn't prepared to have you so *passionate* about it. I went to you and said "teach me," and you certainly did.

I used a questionnaire in the interviews. I wanted to have some way of comparing your answers and I wanted to make sure I covered all the important subjects. One of my temptations was to get so interested in what you were saying that I got off the subject completely. The questionnaire was one way of making sure that we talked about adoption and not the mileage on my Dodge or Sylvester Stallone's new movie.

By the end of November I had finished the interviews and had stacks of questionnaires and rows of tapes. I listened to all the tapes, thought about what you'd told me and started to write.

With eight novels behind me I didn't anticipate any problems. What I hadn't realized was that forty personalities were clamoring to be heard and I felt a responsibility to tell other teenagers *exactly* how you felt, what you said, what you meant. It took a lot of sorting, searching through tapes, thinking, and checking on what you'd said before I could start.

I can't be sure that every one of you told me the truth. I have had a lot experience in interviewing but it is possible some of you could be excellent actors. I don't think so, but, again, as this was not a scientific study that aspect of it was not controlled. It is sometimes difficult to believe that children are subjected to the abuse and neglect that some of you reported. But I know from my experience in community nursing that many children are abused and you know from your own experience or from the experience of your friends that it happens. Adopted kids don't seem to be subjected to any more or less abuse than non-adopted kids. You can probably think of people you know–friends, kids at school–who are abused and judge that for yourselves.

I tried to ignore my own family experience with adoption and imagine questions you might want answered. I wanted to know your needs as you see them: to know about birth parents? to know their medical history? what kind of a family your birth mother came from? what kind of work she did or does? was your father a lawyer? a logger? a drunk? Do you have trouble with the idea of adoption only if you don't get along with your adoptive parents? Or do you have trouble even when the relationship is good? What do you want to know about yourself?

You told me much more than I could have imagined. Your names have been changed but the quotes are accurate. You come from cities, towns and rural areas. You live in many family constellations—one brother, two sisters, no siblings and even four brothers. You have loving families and abusive families, wealthy families and middle-income families. Some of you have left home and are supporting yourselves; some still live at home. You range in age from thirteen to twenty-two. I interviewed you in beautiful homes where Eskimo carvings sat under exquisite paintings and in dark apartments where roommates and boyfriends hung over the backs of the chairs listening and adding comments. I interviewed you in my car, in restaurants, and in shopping malls. You are white, black, Native Indian and degrees and variations of color. Your personalities are as different as your complexions. Some of you were curious and helpful. Others were passionately anxious to tell teenagers through this book what they went through and how they see the problems of their age.

I was prepared to find you polite and a little distant. I was, after all, somebody's mother. So I was pleased and grateful that you were so frank and so willing to talk. Your feelings couldn't be contained in short answers to a few questions. I had prejudices and ideas of my own and you swept them away.

This book took on the form of a conversation with forty of you about your feelings and ideas. Sometimes you told me quietly, sometimes emphatically; but you wanted to tell me and, through me, other teenagers what it is like to be adopted. I became a vehicle of your expression and this book is yours.

1

WHY WERE YOU GIVEN UP?

"What do you want to know about your natural parents?" brought the most definite, quick response. I wasn't expecting your reply and it continued to come as a surprise.

"I want to know why I was given up. That's all." Karen pressed her hands on the table and leaned toward me. "I just want to know why!" Karen dramatized the question that so many had already put to me. She was my twenty-second interview and it was the twenty-second time I'd heard it. It seemed to me that there were thousands of possible answers to my question; "I want to know whether they had any more children," "I want to know whether they're healthy," –any number of things. But as I listened to Karen repeat for the twenty-second time, "Why was I given up for adoption" I finally understood that it *must* be important.

Karen is short, bright-eyed, talks quickly, rushing through a conversation like an enthusiastic evangelist–as if there isn't enough time to tell me everything I should know. She invited me into her large apartment in the suburbs of Vancouver. Her boyfriend and another friend were sitting on the living room rug listening to records; Karen and I sat at her kitchen table and talked. At twenty she's the youngest of five children. The youngest three are adopted but somehow that didn't make it easier for Karen to accept her own adoption. When she learned at age twelve that she was adopted she ran away, but returned. Karen was angry with her adoptive mother for not telling her when she was younger, and she was angry with her birth mother for abandoning her. Her older sister was sympathetic as she also had run away from home when she was younger and returned. She told Karen that she had had the same feelings, but that adoption was something that didn't have to be negative. The sisters talked for a long time but Karen was still left with anger and a feeling of "not being real."

When she ran away, this time at fifteen, Karen hitch-hiked across Canada, returned in a year and then ran away again until finally her dad told her that she would have to leave home. Now, since she has been living on her own, she feels closer to her parents and her brothers and sisters. She understands now that she was difficult for everyone during those teen years with her demands and her questions. Karen still has a tremendous need to find her birth mother. She will not feel like a real person, she told me, until she knows who she was at the start of her life and where she began. When that is resolved she plans to go to school and become a zoologist. But until she settles her beginnings she doesn't feel she can plan anything.

I thought her ambition wasn't practical since she had not graduated from high school but people sometimes do achieve great things from difficult positions and I did want her to succeed.

I kept responding sympathetically to Karen's need to be helped, forgetting that it was her reaction to this need that was paralyzing her. It wasn't the fact of her adoption that was stirring up her life, it was the fact that she thought about adoption all the time and allowed it to interfere with living. I really liked her and I wanted to help her. To her, more than to anyone else I wanted to respond with some positive assurance that she *ought* to know why she was given up for adoption; that in wanting to know her background she wasn't unreasonable, or even unusual. Her reaction was unusual, but her need wasn't. I was overwhelmed by Karen, such an interesting, stimulating person.

The need to know who your birth parents are doesn't seem to be related to how well you get along with your adoptive parents; whether you rate them as good parents, or inadequate parents. Also, your need to know wasn't related to age, sex, or position in the family. Only Ryan and Jo-anne did not think knowing why was of any great moment.

I hadn't thought much about why a child was given up for adoption until I started this project. I had been grateful to the two birth mothers who had given sons to our family, but I hadn't tried to put myself into their minds. I remembered what I had been told about why my sons had been placed for adoption. I had a general idea. Wouldn't that be enough?

Well, not enough for Karen. "I think about it almost every day. When I get all the pieces together, I'll be satisfied. I look in the mirror and think, 'She probably looks like me.' I even asked someone once, a friend of my girl friend's mother, if she was my mother. I knew she'd put a child up for adoption years ago and she sort of looked like me. She said she wasn't and I felt so stupid. I never did that again."

"I think my birth mother was Russian. She might have come over with a group of women that came from Russia to Alberta around that time. They all left again so maybe she's back in Russia. I'll have to go through a lot to go over there and see her. If she's still living there it would be really hard to see her but if she's still here, no problem."

I blinked at that. Was she seriously considering traveling to Russia to find out who had given birth to her? She was. It seemed a drastic, impractical plan.

"Because I was born in Alberta all I have to do is write and they'll send me my mother's name. This doesn't mean I'll go find her. It just means I'm going to know her history and that'll help me out to know things about me that I maybe need to know. I don't know if I'm the same as anybody else and I really do feel lost. I sometimes feel that I don't know who I am. I don't know who I should be.

"Some friends say, 'Oh, come on. I know what it's like.' But no. They don't know. They aren't adopted. Their parents didn't give them up. They didn't throw them out. It hurts you know. I want to know why."

I thought Karen flirted with fantasies about her birth mother. I wasn't convinced that she truly wanted facts. I did believe that she had a great need to know who her birth mother was but that she was afraid to find her. I wondered if it was Karen's intense personality that made the question seem so vital.

Leslie was quite different and yet she had the same need. A queen-sized waterbed dominated the living area of Leslie's studio apartment; pictures and ornaments made it crowded and comfortable. Background rock music drifted from the radio on the kitchen counter. Leslie is a determined, organized young woman with a clipped way of speaking that made me feel as though I'd better be businesslike.

Leslie had discovered her adoption order at age twelve while rifling through her mother's private papers. Her adoptive mother was upset at her discovery; she felt that Leslie might leave her and return to her original parents if she knew she was adopted. Leslie couldn't understand those fears; they seemed silly to her. She had no desire to leave the people she loved to go to strangers, and she didn't understand why that wasn't obvious to her parents. Unlike Karen, Leslie doesn't view her past as an emotional wellspring so much as she views it as a source of information.

That's my impression but Leslie is very self-contained and I couldn't know on one meeting the depths of her emotions. She said that she didn't feel rejected by her adoptive parents; she felt some rejection by her original parents and absolutely no desire to trade homes. Her parents might never have told her she was adopted if she hadn't found out herself. That they were afraid that she wouldn't love them if she knew she was adopted doesn't make sense to Leslie. Why can't everyone deal with life on the basis of facts? Leslie thinks her parents' attitude at the time was wrong but it was their decision. "Mom and Dad thought they were right. They did what they thought was best."

Once Leslie knew she was adopted she started asking questions and, when she was seventeen, started to look for her birth parents. She found her mother's name and got in touch with her sisters. Although she hasn't met her mother, she knows who she is and where she is. Her sisters told her that, of all the seven children, Leslie looks the most like her mother. That pleases Leslie.

"My mom had six children already and her husband wasn't my

father so she had to give me up because she didn't want him to know about me." Although Leslie knew most of her family background, she still wanted to know, straight from her birth mother, why she had been placed for adoption. "My sister didn't tell me much about it but apparently my mother got pregnant from her boy friend and her husband came back. So my mother couldn't tell her husband she was pregnant. So my mother gave me up for adoption. Her husband was so mean, if he'd found out he'd have killed her."

"It was a small town and I guess some people knew about it. She had six kids to raise and seven would have been a bit harder . . . a single parent working two jobs in a small town . . . and at that time they had to worry about neighbors." Leslie meant that her mother would not have been able to support seven children if she had left her husband and kept Leslie with her. "I still don't know who my father is. The only way I'd find out is would be to go and meet my mother and right now . . . . My sister told her that I'm all right. My sister was upset because she wasn't sure if I was going to upset my mother's life. Her husband would kill her even now. I know a lot about her and it doesn't really matter if I don't meet her. The only reason I would like to meet her is because I'd like to know who my father is . . . and I still wonder why the people that had me before didn't want me."

Leslie had been placed for adoption as an infant, then given up at six months, and placed for adoption with her present parents. "It gets really, really confusing. Especially if you don't have anyone to talk to."

2

WANTING TO KNOW

What were your birth mother's reasons for giving you up for adoption? Your mothers were too young and didn't have the money to support you; your grandparents wouldn't help support you; your father wouldn't help. Sometimes a mother tries to keep her baby for a few month or a year and life gets too complicated, too difficult, too stressful. She is often ignored by her family, cut off from the parties, and the fun, and she's usually poor. When you are sixteen or seventeen yourself it is easier to understand why a young mother would give up a baby. And if teenagers don't know why they were given up, they guess:

"Maybe she was too young."

"Maybe she just didn't want a kid."

"Maybe it was a one-night stand and I was a boo-boo."

"I don't know. No one will tell me. I don't know why or even where I was for six months. No one knows why."

"I guess they were too young, didn't have any money and couldn't handle it."

Some parents (and I'm ashamed to say I was one of them) avoid giving you the reasons by telling you that they sent out an order for you and some unidentified woman did the family a favor by carrying and delivering you–a sort of Sear's catalog. Parents like me imply that your birth mother was never really the "mother." I hadn't realized how unrealistic that was; I hadn't realized that by calling my children's mother "the lady who had you" I was taking away her character, individuality, personality. You told me that you wanted a personal connection with a real past, not with a vague, de-humanized idea. It's hard for you to get a good mental picture of a real person, in a real situation, who actually existed with the limited information, "Five foot, six inches, blue eyes, fifteen years old and fair." Even those of you who have a clear idea and good records that tell you why the social worker thinks you were given up want to hear from your mother just why she did it.

In British Columbia and Nova Scotia some social workers are now asking for a letter from the birth mother at the time of adoption telling her child why she gave her up. Such a letter is supposed to be passed on to the adoptive parents. The information in the letter is to be passed on to the child as he is growing up. Most of you thought it would be great to have that kind of communication. There may be problems. What happens if the social worker doesn't get the letter, if she doesn't pass it on to the parents, or if the parents don't pass the information on to the child?

Almost any information would be welcome to some of you even if you didn't approve of the reason. Many teenagers see their beginnings as rejection by their birth mother. There isn't any doubt that the act of giving a baby up for adoption can be seen as rejection. But that doesn't necessarily mean that your birth mother didn't want you.

It is possible to want something desperately and know you cannot have it; to know it would not, in the long run, be wise. It's reasonable to think that giving up a child is hard. While I was a public health nurse I met no one who was able to give up a child easily. Some cried for days. Some didn't cry at all, but that didn't mean their sorrow was less deep. Part of the problem is that at childbirth your body and your heart are ready to nurture a child and react badly to empty arms. Look at your friends who may have given a child up for adoption. Try to imagine how they feel and you many have a better understanding of your own beginnings.

Mike saw adoption as rejection by his birth mother. He was fifteen years old, quiet, preppie, and polite. He allowed me to interview him in the kitchen of his home as his sister bustled off to work apologizing for being in the way. When the house was quiet and we had talked for a while, I asked Mike what he knew about his birth parents.

"Nothing. Mom and Dad didn't know anything about them. I don't know anything"

"What do you want to know about your natural parents?"

"It would be kind of neat to know why they put me up for adoption." He paused. "And maybe, what ages they are. I don't think I want to meet them again. It'd be sort of scary. I might even know them already."

"What difference would knowing about your natural parents make?"

"It might take my mind off some of the things I've thought about." He looked at me seriously for a few moments and then leaned his head back against the wall. "Like why did they put me up for adoption? Was I bad? Was it because of me?" I was startled and thought that perhaps he was making a joke.

"You think she thought you were bad?"

"Yeah. Sometimes I think that."

Mike didn't seem to be upset by this self-derogatory idea; but I was. "You know, Mike," I spoke very slowly, "it seems unlikely that a week-old baby did anything, *could* do anything to make its mother reject it."

Mike shrugged. "I don't know. Not really."

I tried again. "There is nothing you could have done that would make you bad. I mean a baby is just a baby. There's nothing you could have done that was wrong."

He nodded. I think it was a kind of thanks, a recognition that I had tried to understand. Mike was matter-of-fact about it but I was upset that he could even *think* he was responsible for being given up. Wasn't there some way our society could stop leaving kids with this kind of speculation? Perhaps that letter from the birth mother explaining her reasons might help kids like Mike. Mike still feel that perhaps *he*, in some special way, had made his mother hate him so much he wasn't worth keeping. Perhaps he was so angry at her that he imagined her a cruel woman who would do something so rotten. An older girl asked me much the same thing as Mike had. "Was I ugly, or something?"

I tried to get a better understanding of why a mother would give her child up for adoption. I talked to many mothers at the time of childbirth but I wanted to know how a mother felt years later. I was lucky to get some interviews with birth mothers.

A dark, regal-looking woman talked to me in her city home. "We were engaged, but he gambled. I didn't think I could make enough money to support the baby and I didn't know whether what he and I had was going to last."

They did marry and now have a family. It seemed busy and happy—two little girls and a dog kept running back and forth through the kitchen. When her first child was eighteen she searched, contacted his adoptive mother and arranged to meet him. He visits her occasionally now.

"It's nice that I know him. I always wondered about him and worried. In fact, I got depressed every year around his birth date. Now I know that he has a loving family who brought him up very well. And also I know that I will never really feel like his mother. I gave that position away. I'm glad I've met him, though. I feel better about the decision I made nineteen years ago and I think I've lost my depression." Their reunion reduced her guilt and allowed her to live with herself. Her son discovered where he fit in the pattern of his past.

When the discovery that you are adopted comes at the late age of twelve or thirteen, the rejection by the birth mother seems to be more difficult to handle. Karen learned of her adoption when she was twelve. Leslie also learned late and found it hard to understand. "I cried for a long time. Someone dumped me when I was a baby and I couldn't understand why."

Many of you told me that most of your resentment is directed, not at your birth mother, but at your adoptive mother (not your father) for not being honest with you. You trusted your (adoptive) mother to care for you and when your mother withheld important information, you felt betrayed. She was supposed to love you and she lied.

Most of you feel that this information is your right. You feel adoptive parents are not fair or honest when they keep information to themselves. And, as Leslie said, "So what's the big deal? It's my background, isn't it?"

Those of you who knew about your natural parents seemed to be glad to tell me what you could. You saw yourselves as coming from one place and moving to another. Those who didn't know saw the time before their birth as a mystery. Am I the child of a celebrity who was forced by her career to abandon me? Is the woman who works at Eaton's downtown my mother? She looks like me. Is that woman coming down the street my birth mother? Was I born at all or did I just arrive? You don't seriously believe you came from outer space but your joking comments show you are uncomfortable, a little afraid of what might be. You wonder and you worry and you imagine the best beginnings you could have had, and the worst.

Leslie insisted that I understand. "Like you walk down the street and you see someone with brown eyes and brown hair and you wonder, 'Gee, I wonder if they could be related to me?' You could walk right up to your mother. There was one time . . . a girl in a drug store walked up to me and said, 'You know what? If you had your hair cut the same way as my sister you could be identical twins.' And *that* made me think. I wonder if I've got brothers and sisters. They could be right here under my nose and I'd never know it. 'Wanting to know' is just a kind of a feeling. Like there's a piece of the puzzle missing. Good or bad, you are compelled to know. "

"That [knowledge of her birth parents] is part of me. That's part of my life. Whether I was too young to remember or not . . . I was born in that hospital from one woman and I was given to another. That's . . ." Her voice drifted into silence. Then she just said, "and I just wanted to know why."

I thought about why we, society, haven't kept the information for you. There were reasons: former attitudes; the real and imagined desires of both birth parents and adoptive parents. I remember that the lawyer asked me if I wanted to know the name of my son's birth mother. *I* didn't want to know. I was young, insecure self-protecting. It didn't occur to me at the time that my son might want to know and, by then, the information would be lost. All of society that is affected by the laws concerning adoption, except the adopted baby, helped shape those laws. Our understanding of your needs was imperfect.

3

YOUR PARENTS' NEED TO ADOPT

What motivates people to bring a stranger's child into their home? Do they love all children, or anybody's child, or just this child? Many times you told me that the adoptive mother couldn't have children. "My mom has some kind of a problem and she couldn't have kids and they wanted kids so they adopted."

Sometimes parents wanted a particular sex and didn't want to take a chance. "My mom and dad wanted a boy." "My mom and dad wanted a girl."

I was told once by a Native Indian social worker that adoptive parents should make sure that they aren't adopting a child to show their families, their neighbors, and society how kind and generous they are; that they aren't using this child as a way of improving their own social status.

At first, I thought his suggestion ridiculous but the more I considered it, the more I realized some people might feel that adoption is expected of them. Some religious groups encourage their members to adopt children to bring up in their faith and give social prestige to those parents who do so. But even in situations where the motive for adoption is complex, and not just a simple matter of giving love to a child, the children are most often loved for themselves. It is difficult for anyone not to love the child who becomes part of their life, perhaps especially, a child who is difficult and gives a lot of trouble.

Karen's reason was unique. "My mom had twenty-nine foster kids. I was one of those, and she fell in love with me and adopted me."

I remember wanting more children. We had one daughter and were unable to have more babies. We felt our family was too small and we wanted boys. It seemed really quite simple at the time. I don't think I had a reason so much as I had an emotional need. I know that until our last son was born, I felt our family wasn't finished. In both cases, we waited nine months from the time we applied for our son and the time he was born so the whole process seemed quite normal.

I'm sure there are parents who adopt children for reasons other than just a feeling that they want a child. Some couples may feel a baby will hold their marriage together; a baby might make them feel more important, more secure; a baby might make up for the faults of an older child; a baby with special problems needs them.

Kerri said, "Another lady was taking care of me and my mom went to see me and I was lying in this buggy. I was six months old when my mother found me. If she hadn't taken me then I'd have died of pneumonia. I lived in a buggy – that was my crib, that was my playpen, that was my bed, that was everything. I never had any exercise. Every time I cried I guess the foster parents fed me. That's all they did. To shut me up they just fed me a bottle of milk or a cookie or something. So my mom saw me and she just said, 'You poor little thing. You come to me.' Like my mom had two boys and two more boys she'd adopted and she'd always wanted a little girl so she got me. I guess she wanted the experience of having a daughter."

As a young child, Kerri slept in a bedroom above the family living room. Her parents were unaware that she could hear, from her bed, every word they said below her. That was how she discovered that she and her brothers were adopted. It was exciting and special information that she immediately shared with her brothers. Their parents then talked about adoption with them and the subject has since been easy to discuss. Kerri doesn't feel any great need to find her birth parents. She's thought about searching and talked to her brothers about it but she has decided not to look. She feels happy, secure and loved by her family and her boyfriend and she doesn't see any need to disturb that.

Kerri invited me into the house where she was babysitting. She was just nineteen and planned to go back to school as soon as she could, get her grade twelve and then attend a child-care program at the community college. In the meantime, she supported herself with some help from her parents. Kerri is bright and pleasant, and she tried to find subjects she and I could talk about. She wanted to know me and like me and she wanted me to understand her. She told me about her struggles to be independent at sixteen; how she wanted to live apart from her family, wanted to see them only occasionally, wanted to know her own mind, trust herself. But these were struggles to become a separate person, struggles she had in common with other teenagers, not struggles against her adoption or with the idea of being adopted. Now she lives easily and happily in her parents' home, feels like an adult, feels accepted and loved.

She told me about her first conversation about adoption. "Mom and Dad sat us down all together and explained it to us. It felt odd at first. We all felt really strange and really different and we didn't know if we should tell our friends. We thought, 'People are going to say, Ha Ha! You're so ugly your mother didn't like you!' But as we grew older and I told my friends about it, a lot of them said that they would like to be adopted because then they'd *know* that someone really wanted them. And that's how I feel, and that's how my brothers feel too, that our parents really want us. Up to about grade five, I thought my brothers and I were the only ones who were adopted and it felt really good when we realized that other kids were adopted too. I think you should tell the kids that read this book that you think you are the only one – but you're not."

Kerri had the security of four older brothers, two of whom were in the same position of having been adopted into the family. She *knew* she wasn't the only one, or even one of the few adopted ones. It is harder for you, if you are an only child or the only adopted one in the family, to get Kerri's perspective. Kerri's boyfriend sat in the kitchen while we were talking and was occasionally consulted when Kerri wanted to check a date or a fact. They were thinking of marriage and Kerri had a few questions she wanted answered first.

"I'm talking about getting married, so I'm talking about having kids so I want to know medical history of labor and delivery. My mother said they would have told her if there was anything wrong. So no information means no problems."

That's how Kerri looked at it but I don't think she can be so sure. In the past, medical science knew less about hereditary diseases than they do now and medical histories didn't include information that might now be needed. You have to view your own history from the perspective of thirteen to twenty years ago when a medical history wasn't considered as important as it is today. A medical history taken today on a baby and considered detailed and complete might not be good enough twenty years from now. We don't have enough knowledge to ask the right questions.

"If my brothers and I want to find our birth mothers my mom said she'll find out the information and tell us where to call. My brothers and I, we talked about this because we've seen shows on T.V. about kids trying to find their parents and parents trying to find their kids. But we feel that our parents would be really hurt if we tried. As far as we're concerned, the parents that brought us up are our parents and we feel they'd really, really, be hurt. I don't really care if I find out who they [birth parents] are, but if I ever do . . . . My mom says that as far as she knows, my mother is dead and my father is dead also. But I think they have families. Right? I don't think I'd go out of my way to find the family but if by chance I did find them, I'd like to know what my mother was like, or my father. Were they nice people, you know?"

Me: "What difference would knowing about your natural parents make?"

"It would solve this mystery of my background. Do I look more like my mother or do I look more like my dad? It's, like, real weird because when my boyfriend first was introduced he said you *can't* be adopted because you look like your [adoptive] mother. Like I spent my life with her and I have her habits. I have her voice.

We all have dark hair in my family. All wear glasses. Have the same facial features. My brothers all sit and angle their heads and smile the same way my dad does. We look like we have to be related. Back then, I guess, they tried to match you up."

To some extent Kerri was right about that. Society, not just social workers, but parents, ministers, psychologists thought that it was important that you look like your parents. I remember nineteen years ago, a couple went to the hospital to pick up their healthy, newborn adopted baby and would not take her home because she had blue eyes. They wanted a brown-eyed baby so she would look like them. I wonder if they are still waiting for the perfect child.

"I guess I'm always curious as to what my mother looks like. There's a piece missing. My real mother gave me a doll [at the time of adoption] and my mom gave it to me last Christmas." Even though Kerri didn't want to search for her birth parents she held warm to her heart the gift from her birth mother.

"If I never meet them [birth parents] it's not going to bother me. I'd like to know why she gave me up. Not an explanation or an excuse exactly, just why. I would talk to my birth parents if I ever met them but I'd feel resentment toward my mother. 'Why couldn't you keep me?' I guess it's okay. I've spent nineteen years without her and I've turned out pretty good."

In four of your families you had sisters and brothers much older than you. Paul explained, "My parents already had raised my brother and sister and they thought they'd like to do it again so they adopted my sister and me."

In one case, the baby replaced a child who died. "My parents had a son who died. They heard I was available so they picked me up." Dan seemed to think that gave him a ready-made place in the family.

And then there were teenagers who didn't remember why. Fourteen-year-old Judy didn't think it was important to know why she was adopted. "I can't remember why. Mom told me but I can't remember."

In two cases, children were placed by social workers with families who were not ready to love them. For reasons never explained the social worker made bad placements. As in all professions not every worker is excellent. Some social workers make mistakes, some are beginners, some are overworked, some don't have the education they need to make the decisions they must make.

I drove an hour into the suburbs to talk to Dora. She was alone in her boarding house in the well-kept suburb of a small city. Dora is eighteen, living with support from the welfare department, supplemented by babysitting and occasional jobs. She has dark hair, dark eyes and a low musical voice. She had a logical measured way of speaking–didn't hurry but said what she meant thoughtfully and carefully.

Dora knew her birth mother had been young and unable to care for her but she did not know where she had lived before she was placed for adoption at six months. Her adoptive father was a professional man who was away much of the time and her adoptive mother, while home with her, was unable to love her. At twelve years of age Dora faced her mother's indifference and had to learn, after years of hurt and unsuccessful effort, that she couldn't change the situation; she had not caused it. Her mother's rejection was not Dora's fault. That's a tough emotional fact that some adults never resolve.

I had a lot of admiration for Dora. By the time she was fourteen, she knew she could never be loved at home. She was placed in a foster home until she was seventeen, a good foster home with a loving foster mother. Psychiatric counseling helped her to accept the situation. She seems calm and stable now, a mature eighteen. She blames her parents but she also feels sorry for them. Her adoption was an unlucky deal. She was dealt parents who couldn't love her–that's the way the cards fell, that's the hand she had to play in life.

At seventeen when her foster mother was ill, Dora was placed back home by a different social worker. Not a good decision. There she endured physical and emotional abuse for eight months before she moved to a boarding home. Dora wants to work in Early Childhood Education where she plans to help children have a better childhood than she did. She impressed me as a survivor who was not looking back for a reason to fail.

It had taken her years to understand why her (adoptive) mother couldn't love her. "My mom had five miscarriages. Then they adopted a girl who died of a heart condition, then they adopted my brother, then two girls. One died of a respiratory problem and the other had cerebral palsy and they put her in an institution. And then they adopted me."

I found it hard to believe that one family could be subject to such heart-ache. But it is possible that the other children were placed in temporary care as foster children. That might be why so many different placements were made.

"At that point as far as I'm concerned my mother's mental health must have been all down-hill. The social worker couldn't see that. She never re-evaluated the home. She just went on her first assessment way back and never saw what it took from my parents to have all these children come in and out of their lives. By the time I came along my mother was afraid to love any baby; she just froze. Basically, well really, my mom told me that the reason she never really got close was so that, if I left or something happened to me, it wouldn't hurt her."

Me: "So it was a self-fulfilling prophecy?"

Dora: "Yeah. Bonding never really started. My family really broke apart when I was twelve. I've been in and out of foster homes since I was fifteen. "

"My mother told me that my birth mother was raped. She said I was a rapist's child and that was why I had no heart and no feelings. And I believed that. It wasn't until I got my non-identifying information that I found out that my birth parents had been going together for a year and a half." Suddenly her voice got hard as she tried to hold back her pain. "Well, Mom, it was a really long rape; it was a year and a half."

The hair rose on my arms, I felt the muscles of my neck stiffen and I was suddenly furiously angry at her mother. Many of you did this to me. As a public health nurse I saw children subjected to cruelty, neglect and even persecution, but I have never accepted it. It always makes me angry. I reminded myself that I was only supposed to record Dora's feelings, not my own. The silence lengthened.

Finally I said, "Well, you know, . . . that's a *cruel* thing for a mother to say."

Dora let out a sigh. "I guess so. When I asked her why she had told me that I was a rapist's child she said that my mother was fifteen and my father was eighteen so it was statutory rape. Like legal rape. My mom knew they had been going together for a year and a half. She only told me that to hurt me. "

"She upset me for a long time, though. I was trying to make some sense of life and going to school and all that but I didn't think there were any feelings in me or for me at home. But I got help. My English teacher at school sent me to the doctor and he sent me to a counselor and I went for three years because I was really disturbed. It really bothered me – that my mom didn't love me. After two years of counseling the psychiatrist tried to tell my mother what the problem was and she wouldn't listen. She walked out. I tried to get re-united for a year after that, but the psychiatrist said to give it up and try to shape my own life without them. The last time I saw them was two years ago. I was asked more or less not to contact them."

"It hurts, does it?"

"Yes, it does."

"You have to understand my [adoptive] parents. My mom was Jewish and she grew up in a concentration camp in the Ukraine. My dad was German and he was in Hitler's Youth. She saw her whole family getting slaughtered. He was more or less abandoned."

I checked back to see how old she had told me her parents were. It was possible. They would have been teenagers during the Second World War.

"They told me, 'We made it through the war; we made it through. You should be able to make it too.' There was emotional and physical abuse too. But it's two years later now and I feel sorry for them."

Me: "Why did they want children?"

"It's the little dream they had–the mother and the father. So it was the dream of having a little boy and a little girl and dressing them up and having a family and making everything complete."

"What about you? Are you looking for another family?"

"No. I'm not looking for anyone to take me away from this awful world and take care of me. I'm past that. I've got my own life now. I'd like to meet my birth parents. I read the paper for ads about me–looking for information. But I don't expect anything. I don't expect my birth parents to be any particular social class. I'd just like to meet them. It would make me feel secure in myself. Give me an identity."

I felt a warm admiration for Dora and I hoped she would get the information she wanted. I wished I could be a good fairy and throw happiness and bliss her way, but I had too much respect for her hard-won independence and emotional maturity to say so. Dora was looking for no favors.

Sarah, nineteen and indulged by loving parents, had almost a fairy tale experience. She told the story of her parents expectations with pride. "My mom and dad couldn't have children and they wanted them really bad. They had a nursery set up for two years before they got me." Sarah was happily married now and still fondly attached to her parents. I was glad to talk to Sarah. So many of you had difficult lives that I was relieved that someone had had a happy childhood.

Lena also had good feelings for her parents. She felt they had searched for her. "My parents wanted a baby that had one white parent and one black parent – like them. They waited for woman to have this baby and the baby turned out to be blonde and blue-eyed. They said, 'No way.' So they looked around until they found a baby that had a black skin and that was me."

The reasons are varied, but in all cases but two, the parents for one reason or another truly wanted a child at the time of adoption. Almost uniformly the parents were middle to high income earners. None of you were adopted into a poor family; none of you had ever worried about getting enough to eat. All of you, including those of mixed race and those who didn't know what race you were, felt that you belonged to the social group you lived in. All of you feel a strong sense of identity with your crowd, your family, your community. "I wouldn't want to be anywhere else," seventeen-year-old Nicole told me. "I mean, I don't want different friends or a different school or a different family. Nothing else would be mine."

There were two exceptions. Suzanne, age fourteen, wanted another chance with another family. "I'm not loved here. Something else, some other home, might be better. I don't get along with my mother. My mother has unreasonable rules; not normal rules. I hardly get along with either of my parents. They sort of treat me like a stranger – like I'm not really theirs. They treat my brothers like angels. Maybe my birth mother might want to see me."

I interviewed Suzanne at the beginning of this project. She had the first unhappy family situation. Her life was sad, especially since she could see no future there. I had talked to her mother first and been told all that was wrong with Suzanne. I got the impression that her mother felt she had done her best with Suzanne and failed, so there was nothing more she could do. At fourteen? Just when a girl needs her mother? Suzanne's problems seemed deeper than the usual "Mom is so ignorant" attitude that is common to thirteen and fourteen-year-olds. Because I didn't know the family well I could not be sure if my impressions were accurate. However, I got a great sense of sorrow from Suzanne. She did not feel loved.The important question seems to be whether you feel wanted now – whether you are loved and valued now – not what your parents reasons for adoption were. Some of you have a clear understanding of why your parents adopted you, either for good reasons or bad; some have no idea. Most of you showed little interest in your parents reasons.

4

HEREDITY

What makes you what you are? Do the genes and characteristics you were born with make any difference to your life? The fact that you're female or male, so tall, have certain skin color, good eyesight, crooked teeth? Or are you yourself because your environment molded and shaped you like the waves shape a shoreline? Are the only influences in your life your adoptive parents, your four sisters and the city where you live?

It is impossible to decide exactly how much heredity affects personality, but you tried to guess. Heredity, you said, affects you, roughly, half as much as environment.

Can you ignore your heredity? Can you assume, as some families do, that all the traits in you that are different from your adoptive family are unimportant and all the traits that are the same are important? In some families curly hair is an embarrassment to straight-haired relatives. If you are the only musician in a family of sport jocks *and* you are adopted, that musical difference seems to accentuate your adopted status. You're not only adopted; you're really different. Some families, and some of you, find that threatening. You find more reassurance in being *like* your relatives than being *different* from them.

Each one of you also needs to discover the differences in yourself. That's what identity is all about – finding yourself, being an individual. What makes you different from other people? What makes you unique? Where do you fit in society? Discovering who you are is all a part of learning how to walk to your own drum-beat; being independent, being yourself, knowing yourself.

Heredity is the curly hair your birth mother gave you, the sex your father gave you, the allergies, the blue eyes, the long fingers. Heredity is black skin, slanted eyes, a small nose. What you are when you are newborn does make a difference to your life. It does matter that you were born a girl and programed to become a tall woman with excellent health. Your life would be different if you were programed to become a short man who suffered from allergies. It might not be better or worse; but it would be different. It does matter if you were born a boy with brown skin into a society that still equates skin color with character traits and political ideals. Heredity is not as important, you told me, as how you are treated, what your family is like and where you live. But still, heredity is a real consideration.

Cindy-Lou is thirteen, a precise and organized thinker. When I interviewed her in her suburban home her mother welcomed me, then disappeared into the back of the house while Cindy-Lou and I talked.

Cindy-Lou knew quite a lot about her birth parents; what they looked like, ethnic background, talents. "My mother liked to play the guitar and piano and sing. She's just like me." She told me that environment affected her life about sixty-five percent and heredity about thirty-five percent but she still wanted to identify with her biological background.

"When I'm eighteen I want to try and find them [birth parents] and just meet them and stuff. Find both. See what they're like. I've always wanted to meet them. Do they have any other children now? It won't make any difference to my life really. It'll just satisfy my curiosity. I don't know how to go about finding them but I'd love to do it. I'll ask my [adoptive] mom to help." Cindy-Lou saw her adoption into her particular home, her school, and the neighborhood she lived in, as a gift given to her by her birth mother. "I'm not any more special or any less special because I'm adopted. I'm just like other kids. Kids don't believe this 'very special bit.' Maybe I'm a little bit spoiled. My friends say I'm a bit spoiled."

I had a problem with the question of heredity. I realize that a baby comes with genes that are programed for specific talents, body appearance, disease, perhaps even character traits. I've always thought it the job of parents to encourage the good traits and discourage the bad. It didn't make too much difference to me if the undeveloped combination that came in a baby came from my background or not. I have enough peculiar relatives in my history to keep me from being too sanctimonious. But I did think that, as a mother, I had to teach my children how to develop their talents. When my father-in-law told me that my three-year-old son kept time to the music because "Indians have a natural rhythm," I almost hit him. I'd spent three years singing to the kid; he had his own record player and records; I held him up to the piano as soon as he could depress the keys. While I was willing to admit that he might have arrived with the germ of musical talent I refuse to think that I wasn't part of its development.

Many of you have no idea what your birth parents look like. You have no information from the adoption agency and your adoptive parents can tell you nothing. Some adoptive parents carefully collect every scrap of information they can for the child and others (like me) even lose the information they did have and have to painstakingly try to dig it out when the child is a teenager. Many of you have a great curiosity to see your birth mother and to see how much you and your parent look alike. (For some reason undiscovered by me, you don't have the same curiosity to see your birth father, with the exception of Ryan who wanted to know if his birth father was psychologically normal.)

"Who do I look like? There must be somebody out there I look like." Whether or not you have a good description of your birth parents given to you by an adoption agency, you still want to meet your birth mother, to see what she looks like; and you still want to know how you fit into a biological family.

Jo-anne is eighteen, blonde, blue-eyed with a delicate face. She is uninterested in her birth parents history but, "I'd like to know what she [her birth mother] looked like. And her medical history. That's all. It wouldn't make any difference really – meeting her now. It would satisfy my curiosity, I guess, but it wouldn't change anything. I don't care about it really. I'm lucky I'm here. "

"I'm not sure I really want to see her. Maybe. I'd like to see him [birth father] though. I'd like to see if he's good looking."

Jo-anne truly does not care about her birth parents or their history. Although she does read the "Information wanted" column, and the personal ads in the newspaper, she was not interested in any more active searching. As one of two teenagers who did not want to know why they were given up for adoption, Jo-anne was satisfied that the best had been done for her eighteen years ago. "I mean, it's pretty obvious why. She was sixteen."

The only problem she had was enduring taunts from other teenagers. "They bug you – like you're an accident and all this stuff. It hurt sometimes, especially when I was younger. It made me feel as if I wasn't really supposed to be on this earth; but I've learned not to let it bother me."

I had expected some of you to ask about your ancestors several generations back but none of you did. While you were avidly curious about your birth mother, you didn't care very much about searching back any further into your past. You seemed anxious to establish yourselves into a normal, biological family *one* generation back. Not that you wanted to live with that family; you just wanted to know that you began there. You wanted your original history to give you a sense of belonging to the human race; to feel that your thread of life connected with the fabric of everyone's life. Charlie was ironic. "I mean I'd like to know for sure that I didn't come off a tree or something. Did I come into the world normally the way everyone else did?" He knows he did, but he sometimes wonders if the society realizes it.

Paul is dark, energetic, friendly and keenly interested in the whole idea of adoption. He took a lunch break from his work as a hairdresser and gave me the interview in my van, parked on the street. He is nineteen, the youngest of four children and seems secure in the love of his adoptive parents. His brother offered him a good opportunity in his beauty salon and Paul is enthusiastic about his future there. Paul's parents are a hard-working older couple – his father is of retirement age, his mother fourteen years younger. Paul feels a strong sense of belonging in his family, in his religious community (Baha'i) and in his town.

Paul knew that his birth mother had tried to keep him with her for about nine months and then finally placed him for adoption. He was told that he was in and out of ten foster homes before his adoptive parents took him at age twenty-two months. He has no idea why he was passed around so much as an infant. He lives on his own now and gets along well with his family. He sees his growing up years as average, stable, with petty little differences with his parents that don't seem important now. His parents give him advice and encouragement when he asks for it. Paul is not financially supported by his family but the family definitely feels a moral responsibility to him, and he to them. The family is a mixed race family. Paul and one sister appear to be Native Indian; his older sister is white, her husband, black.

Paul is curious about his birth mother but is not willing to risk his present secure family ties just to satisfy his curiosity. His ambitions are not centered on his beginnings but on his future. He plans to be a hair stylist – a good one – "world famous."

He would like to know more about himself. "I mean a little racial history would be nice," he said. "Am I Native Indian? Italian? or what? I don't have a clue. I should know that. My future *children* should know that. I look different from my brothers. A month ago I realized that I'm not like everyone else. That I'm not a white guy. At least, I don't think I'm a white guy. It was just so weird. The only way I see it as different is physically different. Like my brother and I look different. I really noticed it this summer because after the first two weeks in the sun I'm black like a berry. So it's strange. But I don't consider myself mentally different or anything like that. Or culturally different. I've even pulled out my I.D. to prove I'm my brother's brother. But, as a matter of fact, I look like my two sisters [one adopted sister, one natural sister]. We all look alike. Really dark hair, really dark eyes, dark skin. But my brother [a natural child] is the one that looks different."

Others had similar problems concerning race. Bill told me, "I don't know if I'm sort of Chinese, or Indian or what? No one knows. No one's telling me, anyway. I'd like to know where I came from, even if my parents were running drugs. It would be better than not knowing."

Those of you who have information on your natural parents told me with a kind of pride, "My mother was tall and had hair like mine." You also gave your racial origin, "I'm Russian, actually," as if it was a label that established some kind of identity for you. We all spend at least some time as a teenager trying to figure out who we are, how we feel about life, what values and actions are right for us. Feeling that you belong in this family, in this school, in this community and in this human race is part of the task of the teenage years. It's normal to want to know how you fit into life.

Some people argue that you should not know your beginnings because some of those beginnings are unhappy. Most of you have friends who are living with a divorced mother because their father is an alcoholic, or he has moved in with another woman; or you have a friend who is living with her father because her mother left the family. Dealing with trouble, learning to live in a loving relationship even when rejected by one parent, and learning to like yourself, are part of living in society today. You tell me that you can handle your slice of life as well as anyone else.

Most of you were not concerned that you have very little information on your medical backgrounds. All of you had been told that your parents were in good health. It seems unlikely that *all* the parents of so many of you were without *any* medical problems and more likely that the reporting of your medical history wasn't accurate. One of you was born prematurely, one of you had pneumonia, but the rest of you seemed to have had a disease-free background . . . with one exception. One teenager knew that a grandparent had died of cancer.

At the time you were born, most of your birth parents were under twenty-five. Many of *their* parents were under fifty and no medical history was obtained further than that generation. Heart disease, cancer, adult diabetes, cataracts and various other hereditary ailments most often develop after fifty years of age. Only Leslie and Nicole wondered if their history had been accurate.

Most of you didn't question your medical history and weren't interested in it, but some did admit that it might be a concern when you were older. One young woman who had been trying to have a child wanted to know her birth mother's child-bearing history since her own doctor kept asking her for information she didn't have.

"Everyone else has that kind of information. Why can't I have it? What is it? Some kind of big secret? Or is it so bad that someone, somewhere is keeping it from me?"

Two of you (young women) had been told that your mother had died in childbirth. You wondered if the cause was something hereditary – if you, too, would die in childbirth. You couldn't get help with this fear, couldn't decide if it was a real danger or an imaginary one, because you didn't have enough information. You weren't even sure your mother had died; but you were afraid.

While the adopted child becomes, at the time of adoption, a child of the new family "for all purposes" you were still born, of different parents, with a heredity that is all your own. To deny that is to deny reality. To pretend that you started life with the adoptive family is to pretend that you had no prior existence and, while that is not true, many families seem to spend time and energy trying to make everyone believe it. The efforts of society to "match" a child's physical appearance to those of the adoptive family may have been part of this effort to deny their different beginnings.

Those of you who try to recognize that you had a nine-month existence someplace other than with your adoptive family are sometimes frustrated by adoptive parents who deny it, by social welfare systems that withhold information on it, and by some legal systems that seal the adopted person's previous records and refuse by law to allow an adult to find his birth name.

This blank beginning is frustrating. As more and more adopted children grow into adulthood, as more and more become confident about their rights to the same knowledge as the rest of society, more changes should occur to make such simple information as social and medical history automatically available. If we recognize that medical information taken at the time of birth may not be adequate in later years, and understand that genetic history may become of greater and greater importance, we may need to devise some system of filing and retrieving information that would serve the needs of adopted people.

As an adoptive parent, I would like to have had more social information for my sons. I would rather give them information over the years than have no past information or have it come suddenly at age nineteen. I want them to be used to their history and comfortable with it.

One day at lunch with friends we talked about cultural influence. My friend told us how much she had absorbed of her Ukrainian heritage.

"What's your background?" my friend asked me.

"Scottish."

"And mine's French," my son said.

"Why different from your mom?"

"I'm adopted and I was able to improve the family a little."

He does add interest to our family. He should be comfortable with his identity.

It is normal and reasonable to want information. Most of you understand the risk you take in searching for a birth parent. Newfound birth parents may not like you, may not want to speak to you, may not want to acknowledge you in any way. Or they may want to involve you in a life-style you don't want.

Ideally, you want all the information you need without having to search for it. You want access to it at any time, or have it available to you at an early age as you need it.

5

ENVIRONMENT

So what's environment?: the air your breathe, the world you live in, your community, your school, your family? The blanket that cushions, comforts, restricts and irritates you? Environment–a cloak of circumstances, happenings, relationships and limitations – comprising all the woven patterns of the world.

I wanted to know if you thought it was important. Did you think you were predestined to be a certain person? Or did you think that your environment made you what you were?

Kerri tried to explain environment to me.

"Like you're constantly . . . . Everything is coming at you and you're . . . . Its like you're constantly *swallowing* what everybody does, and everybody's habits and the effects and their abilities and everything . . . . And it affects you in every way. Like you know you're brought up in a religion and that's the way it is; and if you're brought up . . . you know, on one side of the street compared to the other . . . that's it. It just all depends on what's around you. Like if you're brought up to do something"

She leaned forward in the living-room chair and tried to make me understand what she was thinking. She had worked out in her mind what it meant to be independent, autonomous and satisfied with herself.

"Like somebody could tell me what to do. People can give me their opinion and I can do it if I want to or not. When I was a kid, my mom and dad said that I had to do what they said, because I was a kid. But now I'm an adult [nineteen] they say I have to decide what's right for myself. Like I can make my own decision. Like I can do that *I* think is right. And they're the ones that told me how to do that. How you're brought up is really important."

Of course I agreed with her. Most adoptive parents would agree with her. Probably most parents would agree that their children grew up to be decent human beings because they, the parents, spent time and effort teaching them how to make good decisions. Courses offered at night school on how to be a better parent operate on the general principle that better parents turn out better children. Few people today give much credit to the theory that you are born with a certain character and you will never change. Most of us realize that change is constant.

Few people would admit to thinking that a person's life was determined at birth. However, I was surprised when a teacher told me that my bright, achieving, energetic, curious, talented son would not learn anything past ten years of age since, "Native Indians don't learn past grade six, Mrs. Crook." I thought that it might be very difficult indeed for him to learn if she was his teacher so I made sure that she never was. I hadn't realized there was that much ignorance still around. I encountered it again when my oldest son exhibited less than his usual good sense.

"Oh well," said a friend, "he's adopted so I guess it's not your fault."

"There's nothing second-class about his birth parents. His mother was a feisty woman, his father an intelligent man. None of us is responsible for this little caper. He is! He's allowed to make the same kinds of mistakes you did."

One of my visits in Winnipeg was to Lena, nineteen, black, sophisticated and intelligent. She invited me into her parents' home in the university area. Beautiful Eskimo carvings sat under exquisite paintings. Carpets and gleaming furniture created quiet elegance. I took a moment to really appreciate Lena's environment. Her seventeen-year-old brother was waiting upstairs to drive her to work. He also was adopted but was not interested in talking about it. Lena was well-dressed and obviously had an advantaged home. Her mother is white, of French-Canadian ancestry; her father is black, from New York. She has three brothers: the seventeen-year-old upstairs and two older brothers aged thirty-nine and forty from her father's first marriage. Her parents separated when Lena was thirteen; she lives with her mother but keeps close ties with both.

Lena feels loved and accepted by her adoptive mother and father. She can talk easily to her mother, with more difficulty to her father, but knows both parents have helped her and will help her with her future.

Lena doesn't know much about her birth mother. She thinks her birth mother must have cared for her because she sent a tiny hand-knit sweater with her and attached a card that said "To Gloria from your mother." Lena cherishes that nineteen-year-old token of love. She has fantasies about her birth mother just as many of you do. She would like to meet her one day and know her as a friend but Lena doesn't plan her life around such a meeting. She is enrolled in university this fall and feels she has almost unlimited choice in her future.

Lena was anxious to talk about adoption; to feel an affinity with teenagers who need to talk about and hear about adoption. She had thought about the effects of environment and heredity. "We studied this in school; we talked about this a lot. Environment kind of made me what I am—the way I think. But I'm not *the same* as anybody I'm around. I'm not like my parents. I'm not like my brothers or anything. But because I was around them, that's why I am the way I am. For the way I look and the way I . . . that kind of stuff . . . I mean at some point it's got to be heredity. There's no doubt about it."

But you know people say to me that I talk like my mother and I look like her [Lena is black; her mother is white] and I know I don't and I kind of laugh when people tell me that because I think they're stupid. But I know I'm a lot like my parents just from being around them. I have mannerisms the same as they do and things like that. So I think it's almost . . . mostly all environment that tells how a person's life really is. I don't think heredity is that important. I think heredity is unavoidable but not very important.

I met a sixteen-year-old girl by arrangement in a shopping

mall in a city–her choice of meeting place. She is cool and blunt, does a few drugs (she said), finds school too easy and thinks her parents play roles. I was impressed, a little startled, but I persisted. She is thin, dark and speaks in short, clipped sentences, with a habit of suddenly going still as though I had said something fascinating. Her eyes twinkled occasionally as if she found entertainment in my questions and her own answers. The joke wasn't shared between us but she enjoyed herself. She wanted to meet me without her parents' knowledge. I think she had done many things in her life without her parents' knowledge. She was a determined, very intelligent, young woman. "Call me 'Stevie' in the book," she said.

The youngest of four adopted children in her family–two brothers and a sister came before her–she talked about adoption as an accident of birth and of little importance now. Many of you may agree with her. She felt that someone should tell me that adoption was "'no big deal." Her position in the family was clear; she definitely felt she had a right to her adoptive parents' attention and support, and that her place was secure. She felt her parents could have done a better job of raising her but her complaints were about methods of raising children and not physical or emotional abuse. A drawback of her intelligence was her feeling that she was more capable than most people and certainly more capable than her parents and that, although they would help her with her future, she was quite able to manage her own life. She made me nervous. I wasn't that confident at forty.

"As far as adoption goes, it's no big thing. Usually if I say I'm adopted it's nothing big; and if it is something big to the person I'm talking to, they don't believe me anyway. A bad thing I hear about adoption is from all those anti-abortionists, those crazy people that say if you don't want the kid, put it up for adoption. I think that's stupid. If you're not going to have a kid what's the point of going through a pregnancy and then giving it up? But then, if you're a parent and you want a kid, I guess adoption would be good for you. I mean if there wasn't adoption, you'd be stuck, wouldn't you?" Stevie thought of adoption as a real, legal process and that a person who was adopted had a real place in the family. Any other attitude was melodramatic.

Stevie felt she had the same rights in her adopted family as any child would have and that she had the same responsibilities to her parents any child would have. She felt she owed nothing to her birth parents and they owed nothing to her. She wanted to meet her birth parents. "I want to know all about them. I want to know who they are, where they live, what they look like. I want to meet them so my curiosity will be at rest." Stevie had definite ideas on environment. "Well, where you live is one hundred percent. That's the most important. How you look? [heredity] I suppose some people like blondes, right? If you wanted to hire a blonde instead of brunette? Well, I guess it would matter some. If you're a woman instead of a man, I guess that affects you about fifty percent."

If environment was very important to you, I wanted to know what kind of environment you thought you could create for your own families. What kind of future did you think you could see for yourselves? Did you think you could change society's attitudes? Today's marriages often end in divorce. We see step-children in the family, half-brothers and half-sisters, foster kids and kids familiar with day care. Some people opt for casual short-term relationships; and others still try a long-term commitment.

What did you think was coming in your future? In spite of the fact that many of you thought there would be more and more short-term, casual relationships, most wanted a long-term commitment. Even Stevie thought she'd like to try for something lasting. "My own marriage, I'd make sure it was to the right person. If I found the right person right now, you know I wouldn't say 'No' just because I'm not ready . . . I wouldn't marry him right now but . . ."

"You'd keep the possibility in mind?"

"Yeah. I think it's stupid going around with someone for two weeks and then breaking up. I mean, you hardly get to know a person and then you break up. I think marriage should be long term."

"Would you adopt children yourself?"

"Yeah. I mean if I couldn't have a child or I didn't feel like being pregnant, I would. But then, still they're not really like your own, right? Because you're born and kids have aspects of you just because they come from you. I did genetics last year and I know you inherit genes. Oh, the recessive bit, I've got it. The kids might look really different because of the recessive genes. But they might look like you."

Stevie was one of two teenagers who thought that a natural child had a natural affinity for parents. Only one other placed a value on a spontaneous maternal (paternal) relationship. So far, it seemed environment was all important. My next interview took me to a teenager whose environment had not been happy.

I drove into the Fraser Valley to talk to Debbie and was surprised to find myself beside the woods I'd played in as a child. It seemed strange to wander four thousand miles doing interviews and find myself right back home.

Debbie's environment had not been happy. She was adopted as an infant into a family of two older boys. A sister was adopted three years later. From age five to seven, Debbie was sexually abused by her father. She told me that until she was fifteen, last year, she had blocked that out, pretending it hadn't happened to her. Her father was charged twice in court for abuse of other children but was not convicted.

Debbie had lived out of town on a farm and had a horse to ride and remembers some happy times. She was the "perfect daughter" until she was twelve. Most of you seem to manage until the teen years, when life gets rough. Then, "I'd do something wrong—maybe not do the dishes properly or do a half-done job – and they'd start screaming at me and I'd start screaming at them. Until I was twelve, I did everything my parents told me, but after that I decided I'd rather be with my friends than with my parents. I had more fun with my friends. My parents never liked any of my friends. They'd never let me talk on the phone. They tried to control me like I didn't have a life of my own."

Debbie fought with her parents for three years. She ran away several times, was "kicked out" several times and she had problems at school. Her grades were poor and she started smoking pot. She tried to OD once, taking aspirins, and was sick for two days. She tried slicing her wrists, and stabbing herself. Then, just as she turned fifteen, she ran away. She had had a plan that she would run to California or commit suicide. The suicide attempts didn't work so she was heading for California. Twelve miles from home a social worker stopped her and put her in a group home and, from there, a foster home.

In the last year and a half Debbie has grown up in what she calls a "wonderful *family* foster home" where she feels loved and accepted. She still looks on her adoptive parents as her parents, but ones she can't trust. She feels she's grown up a lot and is now a capable person. "You either develop a compassion for people [after having a rough childhood] or a hate for the world. The ones that develop a hate for the world are bounced from foster home to foster home and into the gutter." Debbie has no intention of sliding into the gutter. She plans to finish school and become a psychologist. She is determined and, with the help of her foster parents, thinks she can survive.

As a public health nurse, I often talked to teenagers who had troubled lives. Perhaps that was why I found Debbie's story quite believable. It wasn't so different from the stories of other kids I'd known. The only difference was that Debbie had also been adopted. The high rate of teenage suicides is a fact, so it is not unlikely that I would meet some teenagers who had been so unable to cope that they had tried suicide.

Rhea also had a hard childhood and had come to her independence at great emotional cost. She has a strong personality with definite opinions on many subjects. She had thought about heredity and environment and their affects on her.

She talked to me in her city apartment, her roommate occasionally adding a comment. "I think heredity affects you a lot. I mean there was no one in my family who was talented in art or anything. And I always drew pictures and it was never supported. I mean nobody ever said, 'Oh that's really a good picture' and stuff like that. So I never pursued it. And then when I found my [birth] mom, she teaches art and she's an artist. And my sister, who is ten now, she's an aspiring young artist. She draws all these pictures and stuff and mails them out to me. And when I found that out I thought, 'Gee I wonder if I'd been living with her [birth mother] I'd have been . . . . ?'

"There's all these 'if's.' I may have had the heredity to be an artist, but I needed the environment to develop it. I'd say environment was the most important. Environment generally influences you a lot and it takes a lot to really break out of a bad environment. You know that where you are is not a good space to be in. And heredity? This would vary from person to person, but it's very important to me. Heredity–knowing what you are. I'd say that heredity is about seventy-five to eighty percent an influence on me."

Roommate: "But that only leaves twenty-five percent."

Me: "That's all right. She's just telling me how important it is to her. She can rate heredity and environment individually. That will tell me how important they are to her."

Rhea: "I guess it depends on if you know your family was really traditional and all that. I mean you could have missed out on highland dancing or something if you were placed away from your heredity. Although I think they really tried to match you. Environment influences a person ninety-nine percent. Definitely. It's around you all the time. It's always there."

Rhea had broken away from an environment that had abused her, that made her unhappy, and that offered her little future. She'd met her birth mother and had established her own life independent of her adoptive family and independent of her birth family. She was glad to know her heredity, she felt secure in that heredity, but she was mentally and morally strong because of what she had lived through, of the way she had met life, the environmental fires she had passed through.

I hope it isn't necessary to be abused to be strong. Surely we can come to a good and definite character through loving encouragement. I have no idea whether both Debbie and Rhea were rejected by their parents because they were adopted or because they were too independent, too intelligent, too rebellious. I see teenagers rejected by natural parents: a boy told to go out and "be a man" and come back when he is grown, a girl told to live on the street if she won't conform at home. But I can't say whether rejection during the teen years is any more or less in adopted relationships.

Most of you think your heredity is important and interesting but that your environment is twice as important. It's a subject that could be infinitely debated and we didn't try. You told me that environment is important to you. It is the world around you that makes the difference.

6

YOUR FEELINGS
ABOUT BEING ADOPTED

Most of you saw adoption as a good way to give homes to children who needed them. During the junior-high years, many of you were teased with, "Your mother didn't love you." and "You're weird" because you're adopted. While this teasing hurt at the time, it wasn't the general attitude and the kids stopped using it to needle as you got older. None of you reported problems over adoption with friends or neighbors at the time of the interview. You told me that adoption made no difference to your chances in life or to the way you were treated outside of your homes.

You seemed indifferent to the questions about social prejudice and, since I had assumed you met quite a lot of prejudice, it took repeated answers of "No one treats me any different because I'm adopted. It doesn't make any difference" before I believed you. I couldn't judge social prejudice from my experience with my sons because I knew of few that I thought were prejudiced.

You had few problems with brothers and sisters because you were adopted but two of you told me that you had a grandmother who couldn't accept you as part of the family. In both cases your parents explained that the grandmother was old and wrong. "Grandma's a little crazy; you're all right."

You had friends who were adopted; you had cousins who were adopted, neighbors who were adopted. There are more children adopted today than thirty years ago. I have sixty-five first cousins, none of whom are adopted. My children have fourteen cousins, five of whom are adopted. I took an imaginary flight down the street where I live and did a census. Two of my children are adopted; my first neighbor has three children she bore herself; the next neighbor has one natural child and one adopted child; the next neighbor has one adopted child, then one natural child; the next neighbor has two children that are natural children to her but step-children to her husband.

Families today tend to be combinations of natural, adopted, step and foster children more often than they were, even ten years ago. When you are young, as Kerri said, you sometimes feel you are the only adopted child in the world but by the time you are fifteen or sixteen you know other kids who are adopted.

The adoption process must have some success in your minds for everyone of you told me that you would adopt children yourselves. Some didn't see yourselves in a position to do so for many years yet; some said you wanted to have natural children first. But all said you would adopt. All (expect Suzanne who had mixed feelings) had a positive attitude toward the practice of adopting children. Many felt that you would be better parents to an adopted child than your own had been.

"I would understand," Rhea said emphatically. "I'm going to adopt. And I'm going to foster children too. Because there are just too many children in this world who don't have a decent home or some place to say, 'This is where I can come and touch down when things get too rough.' Anyway I figure I know how to do it. Oh yes. You bet! I'll adopt."

While her ideas were similar, nineteen-year-old Sarah came to her conclusions through a good home and loving attention from her adoptive parents. "My parents did a good job [on me] so I can, too. For sure, I'm going to adopt."

Sarah arranged to see me at her parents' apartment in a busy section of Vancouver close to downtown. She is blond, fair-skinned and the only child of loving parents. She married last year and now lives three hundred miles north with her husband and was visiting her parents for a short holiday.

Sarah knows quite a lot about her birth parents. Her adoptive parents read the social worker's history of her birth parents and remembered much of what they had read. When Sarah was fourteen her adoptive mother told her everything she knew. Sarah knows what kind of a person her birth mother was, where she worked, that she had a sixteen-year-old daughter, what her father was like, what work he did–but not his name. She knows that her sixteen-year-old sister offered to quit school and look after her, that her mother just couldn't support two children and that she had had no one to help her.

Sarah knows her birth mother's name, address and telephone number but she doesn't plan to contact her. She knows her adoptive parents love her. She feels much more comfortable talking to her mother about her adoption than her father because he doesn't like to think of Sarah's beginnings. But Sarah is happy with her start in life. She feels every one has a right to know who he or she is and be comfortable with that knowledge.

She would like to meet her birth mother if that was agreeable to her birth mother but she would not barge into her life without some indication of welcome and Sarah isn't sure how she could find out if her mother wants to see her. Sarah is a married woman now, with some understanding of the choices of women, and she is glad that her birth mother chose to go through with her pregnancy and not have an abortion.

"I'm glad my mother gave me up for adoption. I love and respect her for that and I don't even know the woman."

Sarah has very real feelings for her adoptive parents. She feels that the parent-child relationship is an emotional one that grows and not a biological one that just exists. She feels her parents gave her a good childhood and she looks forward to her future. After she's more accustomed to being married, she plans to attend college to become a social worker. I wanted to know how some teenaged boys felt about being adopted. It might give me some ideas of any differences between boys and girls on this subject. I had the impression, so far, that boys just didn't concern themselves with it very much. I didn't know whether that was because boys generally are taught by our society not to discuss emotions as deeply or as often as girls, or whether they just didn't care as much.

Fifteen-year-old John lives at home with his adoptive parents, two sisters and one brother. No one else in the family is adopted. He is tall, lanky, quiet, a good student in high school and plans to get a law degree. While interested in adoption–he answered the ad in the paper about interviews–he isn't worried about it. He had some information on his background. During the first fourteen months of his life he was placed in several different foster homes. Neither he nor his (adoptive) mother knew why. The curiosity most of you feel about your birth parents is shared by John. He'd like to meet them, see what kind of people they are and find out if he has any brothers and sisters.

John said he would marry eventually and have children. He would adopt children, he told me; he could tell his son what it was like, "I could tell him I went through the same things," the wondering, the talks with his parents. He'd understand his own son's need to do all that. I didn't get any sense that John was anxious and while he did say that he had had concerns in the past and talked them out with his parents, he didn't tell me what those concerns were.

Maryann, sixteen, worked split-shift at a fast-food restaurant and had three hours free before going back to her job. She threw a jacket over her uniform and climbed into my van in the parking lot where we were out of the rain. She was slight, short and spoke in teen jargon that somehow made her feelings seem all the more spontaneous. She was slow to start talking but once she began to tell me how she felt, she talked for a long time without much urging. She had lived through difficult years between thirteen and sixteen, leaving home several times, over-dosing, and generally trying many ways of getting away from her family. She felt anchorless, drifting without direction, floundering around Children's Aid, social workers and her parents. Right now she was trying to get Children's Aid to support her in an independent apartment. She wants to be in charge of her life; she feels she does better when she is living away from authority.

When she is eighteen, Maryann wants to find her birth mother, but not her birth father. Her adoptive parents are willing to help her although her father is worried that rejection by her birth mother will hurt Maryann. Her adoptive mother doesn't think that will happen. She thinks that, since her birth mother kept Maryann for six months before placing her for adoption, she did care once and would probably be willing to talk to her.

Maryann wants to know who her birth mother is and what her name is, but she thinks of her adoptive parents as her parents—even though she doesn't want to live with them. She had ambitions that didn't seem practical to me. If she can make it through high school and get into a university, she plans to be first a medical doctor, then a psychiatrist who works with delinquent kids. "A lot of kids feel that adopted kids are not really people; that's their attitude. They want to know how you deal with being given up. They're curious, I guess. My family treats me okay now. I get some negative feeling from my grandma because I'm adopted. When I was younger that hurt but my mom put her down for it. One uncle and aunt are okay. My friends and neighbors don't care about adoption. They treat me okay. No problem there. "

"When I was thirteen I tried to commit suicide. I guess you could say I OD'd. I took a bunch of pills. I really hated my mother. It was to the point that I really hated her so much that I wanted to get out and get away. You know what I mean? I had a teacher who took me to the hospital. After that I had social workers and psychiatrists and I was knocked around from social worker to social worker and I was starting to hate them, you know what I mean? "

"I've got one at Poplars now that I had from grade nine at St. John's. I mean we just don't get along at all. I sit down and it's the same questions she asks every week. I don't know. It's stupid, sometimes. You see it was strange, because I didn't know I was over-dosing. Like I was just blank. I was taking them [pills] all day; I took them in class. I mean I had them because I was up to ten or fifteen aspirins a day—every day. Plus stress pills. It was kind of like a high all day. It made me relax. Then, after a while I was just taking them and taking them. I had a bottle on my desk and I took all the pills in the bottle."

Maryann sat in silence for a moment and watched the summer rain stream down the front window of my van. "The thing is, now I've got a problem. I'm living out of the house and now I've got to find another place to live. So now I have to go down to Children's Aid again and get mixed up with all their stupid social workers and everything. It's going to be a real pain. I mean, when I was younger I went to Children's Aid before to get out of the house. And what they wanted to do was have a family get together, you know? My dad and my sister were willing to go but my mom wasn't. She said it was my problem, not hers. She didn't want nothing to do with it, eh? So I don't know. It's a money problem now. I can't live off my dad. I don't know what's happening now. "

"When I go I there [Children's Aid] I don't know what they're going to say or what. 'Cause if I go in there, they're not going to shove me in no home." Maryann was flatly determined. "That's for sure. I mean if I go in there and they say, 'Well, we'll stick you in this home,' I don't know, I'd rather live on the streets. It's not as if I'm up to anything most of the time, you know. I mean most of my life now is just working, going home, sleeping, working, going home [to her sister's place], sleeping. So I mean it's not as if I'm up to anything. I'm happier now. For some reason inside of me, I feel a lot better now I'm out of the house."

We watched the rain, cocooned in my van, thinking about the problems of being sixteen. My son David poked his head out of the Dairy Queen. I waved. He ducked back inside.

"Sometimes being adopted doesn't affect my life at all and sometimes it does. You know, sometimes I think, 'When I find her [birth mother] I'm really going to wring her neck. She ain't going to hear the end of me.'" She smiled and shrugged. "Adoption isn't going to affect me. It won't bother me at all. My mom and dad treat me like they would if they'd had me. I mean I *can* go back home. I mean even though she kicked me out, now she doesn't mind if I go back home. But now that I know what it's like being out, I don't want to go back. I've been out of the house two months now—after the end of grade ten. I lived with a friend for two weeks and they were going to keep me, but me and my friend started not to get along, you know how that happens, so I moved in with my sister and now my sister and I aren't getting along. She keeps saying, 'When are you going to move out? When are you going to move out?' I live with her and her boyfriend. My mom doesn't think I'm going to get anywhere. I'm a number one skipper-outer. I don't know, I just . . . . "

"Once I don't go to school for a while, it's just like it's a big problem to me. You get addicted to not going. It's like stealing. I can't go back home now. It's because of the freedom I've known. I can go out when I want to; come home when I want to. But I know I still have other things to do. It's just like being eighteen and moving out on your own type-thing. When I was living at home it was like you stayed in that house and you didn't do this and you didn't do that. Now I'm getting out, doing what I want to do and, you know, school's easier, I go to school when I'm on my own. I was going to school–all my classes–at the end of the school year when I was on my own."

I asked Maryann how she saw her own family future, her own loves. "I think there will be less marriages in the future. I'm going to have a lot of affairs, not just one long-term relationship. Like that's over now. Long time ago you met one person and that was it. You married them. Not any more."

"Would you adopt children yourself?"

"Yes."

"Why?"

"Because I think I'd understand what an adopted child is going through at certain times and ages. Compared to what parents do that weren't adopted. Like my sister [a natural child] wants to adopt. But you know I just hope she'll understand."

David was patiently waiting under the eaves of the Dairy Queen, hands in his pockets, shoulders shrugged high as he tried to keep the rain away from his neck. We felt guilty for being warm and dry, opened the door, called and he dashed through the rain to the van. I forgot to turn the tape off and have a record of David criticizing my driving all the way back to Delores' house.

Some teens were willing either to adopt children or to experience childbirth. Fifteen-year-old Mike told me, "Yes, I'd adopt. I'd like to have a natural child but if my wife couldn't have children I'd adopt. I'd like a baby right after its born. I think it would be hard to have it when it's older because you wouldn't know how it's been treated."

Suzanne, as you may remember, is fourteen years old. Her mother told me that Suzanne was "difficult, . . . a handful." Besides being slim, blonde and beautiful, I thought Suzanne was intelligent and sad. Suzanne found it hard to talk to me, hard to tell me what she was thinking. She spoke hesitantly, softly, taking time between her sentences to decide whether she would tell me at all. She was the youngest in a family of three children, the only adopted child and the only girl. In spite of what ought to have been a privileged position Suzanne felt she was treated as an outsider in her own family. She didn't get along with either her mother or her father and thought that she would never be "good enough" to fit in the family. In some ways, she felt lucky to have a family that could give her food, clothing and an education, and, in other ways, she felt the isolation wasn't worth it. She ran away from home when she was twelve and stayed away for a year. When she returned nothing had changed. She still felt unwanted, unacceptable, not quite what the family expected.

When she is eighteen, she plans to search for her birth mother. She might try to build a relationship with her birth mother since she doesn't see any future with her adoptive mother.

Suzanne often had a different opinion from the rest of the teenagers I interviewed. "Yes, I'd adopt. I'd treat my children as I wanted to be treated as a kid. I'd let them know everything about their parents." And then on second thought said, "But then maybe I wouldn't adopt because I don't want my children to carry the worry of wondering about their natural parents. I don't want that to be between us."

Two quiet sixteen-year-old boys had the same opinions. "If we [my wife and I] couldn't have children, it would be neat to adopt."

Adoption seems to be a reasonable possibility to most of you. Only Suzanne has reservations about her ability as a parent to deal with it. This doesn't mean that many of you aren't independent thinkers. All of you feel that you have come to your understanding of adoption by puzzling it out for yourselves. Adoption is not a subject that's often discussed in the classroom or the school yard except as a curiosity. You don't seem to group together to talk about it. This was one reason why so many were anxious to talk to me; you couldn't seem to talk to anyone else. Even when you felt secure in your own social situation, and even though you felt adoption was a reasonable, realistic social process, you didn't talk about it. Some feel that talking about adoption is somehow "disloyal" or "hurtful" to your adoptive parents. I had thought that my sons didn't talk to me much about adoption because they didn't care about it. But you made me realize that I couldn't presume that. You told me they probably *wouldn't* talk about it.

7

YOUR FEELINGS
FOR YOUR PARENTS

The teenage years are tough years with parents. You told me that your parents were uninformed, too critical, too demanding. But when asked to rate your (adoptive) parents out of ten, (ten was high and one, low) seventy-five percent of the you rated your parents between eight and ten. Twenty-five percent rated your parents six or less. Even those of you who had had stormy years with your parents, who had run away from home or had been unhappy, didn't always rate your parents low. "They really tried," one girl told me. "I was an awful kid. I'm really glad now that I came back and tried again because they really cared."

Karen said of her family, "I get along great with them now. In the past year, now I do. Like now I love them more than ever. When I was fifteen and up to now, I didn't care what they said about my life because they were wrong. Because as far as I was concerned they didn't know me. I felt a natural mother had a certain touch with her own child–like she kind of knew things about her own child. That's what I thought then. So I figured they [adoptive parents] didn't know anything about me and talking to them was a waste of time. And it was a waste of time to me. There's only two people–you and my sister–that I have actually wanted to talk to –wanted to tell these things about adoption. "

"Other than that . . . me and my parents, we haven't sat down yet–to this day, actually–to see how I feel. It was such a huff when

I wanted to find my real mother. No one had the . . . calmness to actually get into a deep discussion with me. So like, my [adoptive] mother told me that because of the fact that I was the last child, and she'd been through so many things with the other four: sex, managing money and things like that, just the ways of life period . . . she didn't talk about those things with me.

"Most children learn from their parents. I didn't learn; so now I'm on my own and I find it really hard to even know budgeting. All I know is the bad things; because I was out there, out in the world by myself. I'm just starting to experience the good things. I'm just starting to get myself on my feet. But still I'm not stable enough. I'm too emotional. Anything just hits me and I blow up like a fire hydrant."

Me: "But, at least you know how to feel."

Karen: "I know how to feel, all right. I'm getting pretty sick of all this feeling. I'm having trouble accepting love, too. I know there's something inside me I have to deal with. Because my own [birth] mother couldn't keep me, I thought she didn't love me. I still think she didn't love me. This is why, when somebody tells me they love me or somebody tries to show me they love me, I reject it."

Karen's boyfriend was listening to records in the living room of her apartment. Karen had an immediate problem with her feelings. She wasn't just projecting that she'd have problems in the future. Her boyfriend was here, and her problem was now. "You know, I need so much proof–unreasonable proof–because of the fact . . . . It all bears down to my mother. That is the problem."

Karen understood with her mind that she was only a baby and couldn't have done anything to cause rejection, but she, like Mike, felt unlovable. "My mother couldn't love me. How can somebody else love me? That's what it is. I've had love and I have love right now. I've just got to accept it. "

"I have to solve this and know the reason why I was rejected. The reason might not be what I want but at least I'll know and it will ease my mind a hell of a lot. If it was money? Understandable. I would understand that. Or if she was going to die in a year. But I want to know. "

"I don't have a lot of self confidence. I'm twenty and I don't even have my grade twelve. If you don't have grade twelve you don't have much self-confidence. I need a lot of people saying to me, 'Oh, you look good.' I need to build my life so I have something to make me feel good. This is why I'm doing this [getting her grade twelve diploma] so I have something to feel good about myself. Now I feel I do everything wrong. Here I am babysitting two kids and when I get angry at them, and I have good reason to get angry at them, I think, 'I shouldn't have done that.' I feel all the time, 'I shouldn't have done that.'"

"When I was fifteen I didn't know where I was heading. I didn't even know who I was. I didn't even know what I wanted in life. I couldn't classify myself as a loser, achiever, average, anything. I wasn't sure about myself. I didn't know what I was, so I couldn't tell you. At school they used to tease me about adoption. But that's junior high school. Kids bug kids. If you're not a good looking kid in school . . . like I hung around with four girls who were models, so I was rated as lower than they were with all the guys. And when they picked on me that's the thing they used against me. 'You were adopted' they used to say things like that. 'Your mother doesn't love you. She's just keeping you till you're old enough and then they're going to throw you out.' All these things were put in my head when I was younger. Maybe that's what started it – my peer group. "

"The good things I heard about adoption I heard from my own sister and brother [adopted also] Sometimes it [adoption] is good. Sometimes there's just no way the parent could keep the child and it's good that there are people out there in the world who will take care of you, you know, instead of having you thrown in foster homes all your life, or being a ward of the government. I thought my relatives treated me differently but you know it was probably just me. I mean I even do that to this day. I see things that aren't really happening. It's just my perspective. I always thought that the natural ones were getting treated the best and we were getting the worst of it all, you know, and I resented it. "

"Because of what I put my mother through my brothers used to call me a 'slut.' They used to call me names. They used to say,

'You don't belong here. Get out of here.' [Two of Karen's brothers were also adopted.] Because of what I put my [adoptive] mother through, they resented me. So it was like me and my own little war against everybody else. The only one who truly understood was my father. He is the only one who has to this day kept by my side and has always called me 'his little baby girl.' Until the day he threw me out. But he was hurtin'. He was crying. He just had no choice. I was a pain. I was really a pain and I want to get over it. "

"My family is very strong, very career-oriented, all of them. They're all affectionate, all loving. My family is super. There's nothing wrong with them – now. When I was giving trouble against my mother, my family was giving it right back. And it wasn't good then. I was a rotten child. I was rotten. I pulled a knife on my brother, like for hitting my sister. Things like that."

I had a sudden surge of sympathy for Karen's parents and looked straight at her. Her eyes twinkled in understanding and she nodded. "I really was a rotten kid. When we were all younger we were all so close in age my mother said this is why we went through all this. The only way I figured I was ever going to get out of my situation was to scrap my way out of it.

"I always figured I was a rebel. I met a lot of people who scraped with me and I wasn't going to be 'Miss Sweetness' and sit back and smile. I was going to scrap right back.

"I think when I ran away from home [at fifteen] and hitch-hiked across Canada I learned a lot – some things good, some things not so good – but I was independent. At that time I was doing what I wanted to do and no one was going to tell me any different and no one was ever going to tell me I was wrong because I never gave anybody a chance. Even now, when someone tells me I'm wrong or somebody tells me I'm doing something wrong, I rebel against it. I say, 'Forget it. I can do what I want. I can say what I please.' My family knows that now. My mom knows that. She will not argue with me now. My own sister, the one that's twenty-seven, takes my advice. I tell her what I think."

Karen was silent for a moment. "I get into trouble that way. I feel terrible about hurting people because of my big mouth. I have to learn not to do that. My family will always be there; they'll put up with that. They give me the time to learn not to hurt them. But with friends? They don't give you the time to learn that. With friends, you say something that hurts them. You hurt them, period. You're through. I always thought that it was okay to say what you thought, but it isn't always. Especially if it hurts someone."

The trouble Karen and her family went through seems to have given Karen a sure emotional support now. "I finally realized that they [my adoptive parents] brought me up. Mom is Mom. My family is super now. My sister talked to me; she said that she went through the same resentment. The feeling of being alone. I mean like, 'Who are you? Your own mother gave you up. What was the matter with you?' She told me that she put my mother and family through hell too. She finally realized that they brought her up; they clothed her and they fed her and they comforted her. The alternative was foster care. At one time she wanted to find her parents but she doesn't even want to meet her birth mother now. Mom is Mom, born through her or not, Mom is Mom because that's who she was raised with. I couldn't understand that then. But I understand it now."

When I asked you to evaluate your parents you were realistic. If you rated your parents below five on the one to ten scale, it was usually for a serious reason such as abuse, or a cold attitude, a lack of caring. No one who was having only the usual problems of interfering mothers, or demanding fathers rated his parents below five, except Katy who told me she was having a particularly stormy time of it with her (adoptive) mother.

Everyone of you felt that your adoptive parents owed the same kind of responsibilities to you as to natural children. There should be no differences between you. Only Suzanne felt that there *was* a difference between herself and her brothers who were natural children. She thought there *shouldn't* be any difference but that there was. No one else saw any differences and no one expected that there would be any differences. Some of you thought your parents needed to be more understanding than most parents and help you find your beginnings: your birth parents or information about them.

"If they accept me as their child, then they accept the fact that

I am adopted and that I have a different history from them. If they accept me, they can't ignore the fact that I'm adopted." Rhea was emphatic about that.

Sarah, who had been given her background by her adoptive mother complete with her birth mother's name, felt that a child had the right to know his own history, and that adoptive parents have a duty to provide this information.

When I asked you what you thought the responsibilities of a child to his adoptive parents were, all of you told me that the child had the same responsibilities as a natural child.

You started life with another set of parents. What are these parents' responsibilities to you?

"They should let me know who they are. Nothing more." Dora had spent some time thinking over the question.

Rhea thought differently. "I think they owe me my background and the reason why they gave me up. At least that. But not their names, or where they live now."

Lena thought the responsibilities of her natural parents were over. "I'm here and that's pretty well all they needed to do for me, give me to a good home."

Leslie said, "My mother owes me something. She should tell me who my father is. If she doesn't want to tell me that's her prerogative. I'm not going to fight her for it. But she ought to tell me." [Leslie, as you may remember, knows her birth mother's name, where she lives and quite a lot about her.]

Katy wanted to know why she was given up. She felt her birth parents owed her a reason. "Not an explanation exactly or an excuse or anything really involved–just why. I also want to know if there are any loonies in the family."

Most of you did not feel that your birth parents owed you anything at all. Nor did you feel you owed anything to your birth parents.

"No, definitely not. No. I don't owe them anything." Only fourteen-year-old Katy felt an obligation to her birth parents. "I owe it to them to grow up to be responsible; to lead my life right. Not to screw up. They put me up for adoption because they didn't think they could bring me up in an environment that would be positive. They put me in a good home and they probably want to see me grow up to be a responsible person."

Rhea also felt that she had a responsibility not to disrupt her birth mother's life. "I should give her a guarantee that I'm not going to cause problems or seek revenge for her giving me up."

Dora said the same thing in a different way, "I feel an obligation to let them live their own lives." No one else felt any obligation to their birth parents.

I asked you what difference it would make to your lives if your knew your birth parents.

Katy said, "I want to know them. More than anything, I want to know who they were; what they were like – their lifestyle; if they are alive. That bothers me, seeing as you have to wait until you're nineteen to find them. That's a long time. It wouldn't make much difference, really, knowing about them. I wouldn't put my parents down – like I wouldn't forget about them and go and live with my natural parents. They're [adoptive parents] the parents that brought me up and they're the ones I'd stay with." [Even though, at this time, Katy thought her adoptive mother was old-fashioned, too strict and didn't understand her at all.] "My natural parents didn't have to put up with me as a baby. They didn't! They didn't have to bring me up. It's the truth."

Paul said, "I don't know if it'd make much difference. I'd like to watch them for a week – be invisible or something so I could see what their life is like without them seeing me. I wouldn't intrude unless . . . I don't think I would intrude. I'd like to know who they are and what they're doing."

Nicole wanted to know, "What they look like and that's it. I would be concerned about invading their own privacy now. I don't think it's important [to meet them] because I know basically the reason I was put up for adoption and I'm quite willing to accept that. No problem with that. But I want to know what they look like. To see why I look the way I do, stuff like that. I was given a description of height, hair color, eye color on the forms but I'd like to see for myself."

Eighteen-year-old Sherry said, "I would like to know about my [birth] mother. I really would. I'd just like to meet her some day. I'd like to know what she looks like. She might not want to see me but if I could just meet her I'd like that. I'd like to talk to her and meet her."

Fifteen-year-old John was systematic about his needs. "I'd like to meet them. See what kind of people they are. I'd like to know their occupations, where they live and what they look like. I'd like to know if I have any biological brothers and sisters and other relatives. It would kill off a bit of curiosity I have about them."

Helen said, "It wouldn't make a lot of difference but it would satisfy my curiosity. If I never met them it wouldn't bother me a lot. It would bother me, say ten percent, but if I met them I wouldn't regret meeting them. It would satisfy me. A lot of it is curiosity: what they look like, who they are, who I look like, who I take after. I'd also like to know my grandparents. I've never really known my [adoptive] grandparents. They both live ... [in Europe]. I only met them twice. And I'd just like to know who my grandparents are. I'd like to know what they're like compared to my parents, compared to me."

Suzanne joined the majority with, "I'd be happier. I have all this curiosity built up about them."

Lena repeated Suzanne's general ideas, "It would give me a history. Let me see where I came from. Satisfy a curiosity."

Rhea did meet her birth mother when she was seventeen, one year ago. She told me the difference it made to her. "It was like this big, huge, ultimate question was answered. It was being able to look in the mirror and being able to identify with someone."

If you did have information about your birth parents, did meet them, or see them, or in other ways feel an identification with them, how would you then feel about your adoptive parents? I asked you, "What would you do if your birth parents came knocking on your door? Not that it's likely. But if, for some reason, they did come to your door, how would you fit them into your life?"

Suzanne was the only one who was willing to consider a parenting relationship with her birth parents. No one else was willing to try to fit their birth parents into his life as some kind of parent-substitute. Many were willing to try to fit them in as friends, or as friends of the family.

Cindy-Lou explained, "I wouldn't go away from my [adoptive] mother but I'd try to be a friend to my birth mother. I guess I'd try."

Lena said, "I think I'd like my birth mother as a friend. Someone who could be a buddy and come over for coffee."

Nicole was more cautious. "If we got along I'd try to treat her as a friend of the family."

Stevie was blunt. "How should I know? They might be idiots."

Sherry said, "It would be hard to do that [fit birth parents into her life] because they'd be no different from any other friend. They were never there in the beginning. It would be really hard to fit them in."

Sarah said, "I'd respect her as a friend, I think. But my *real* mom and dad are the ones I have. I think I'd like to see my birth mother now and then. But not yet."

And Rhea, who knows her birth mother, told me that she sees her birth mother, "Fifty-fifty as a friend and as a kind of a mother. She can't really be my mom. She wasn't there to change my diapers. She wasn't there to make me feel better and wipe off the tears. But now she's there to talk to when I need someone to talk to and I can't do that with my adoptive mom because she [adoptive mom] is just such a judgmental person.... I tried to find my [birth] mom when I was fifteen and being bounced from foster home to foster home. Everyone kept saying. 'You can't find her until you're eighteen' and I kept saying, 'I don't need her when I'm eighteen, I need her now!' I found her when I was seventeen and I'm glad I did. But like I said, she wasn't there in the beginning for all those years and she didn't 'mother' me. She's a friend though."

Mike had a little trouble telling me exactly how he felt, "Maybe I'd fit them into my life as friends. I sure wouldn't kick out my mom and dad, if my real mom and showed up. They put me up for adoption so ...."

Me: "They had their chance away back then?"

Mike: "Yeah."

Me: "And they blew it?"

Mike: "Yeah. This could all be different if I was adopted when I was older. I'd have different feelings about my [birth] parents then. I might have liked them. Or they might have abused me and then I wouldn't like them. I don't know them at all. I don't know if I would want to know them."

Leslie said that she would talk to her birth parents. "I feel resentment to my birth mother. Why couldn't she have kept me? But I've spent nineteen years without her and I've turned out pretty good."

Debbie said, "It would be pretty difficult to fit my birth parents into my life. I don't think I'd want to. I mean I have enough problems as it is. I think a lot of problems would arise from any relationship like that too. I mean Sue [foster mother] has motherly feelings toward me. I mean she's only seven years older than I am but still, she has motherly feelings toward me. And my [adoptive] mother! She'd be really threatened by it. But Sue would understand. She knows I would never leave here to live with either of my parents. She knows that. I've reassured her so many times. We've had a lot of discussions about that one."

"Those two [Debbie's foster parents] would do anything to make me happy. They'd bend over backwards for me, and they have. But I'd do the same for them. Other people would be affected if I started a relationship with my birth mother. It would even affect my relationship with my boyfriend. He thinks it's an excellent idea that I want to look for her but, then again he'd probably get upset if I had any more demands on my emotions." Debbie had looked at how she was handling her life and decided that she could not, at this time, juggle any more relationships, including one with a birth mother.

Helen would like to meet her birth mother and have her as a friend. "She'll never be a parent but it would be nice to have her as a friend. I was really upset when I was about thirteen. I wanted to meet my birth mother then. My [adoptive] mom did a lot. She talked to me. She did try [to find her birth mother]. That helped me the most. My [adoptive] mom cared enough to try and help me go through the pain that I was going through then. I used to see those television shows like 'Little House on the Prairie' where they made adopted kids seem sad, pitiful. Like who was going to take care of them? That got to me. Probably I just wanted to be hugged by Mom [adoptive mom] but I thought I really did want to know more about my birth mother."

Me: "Do you think it would have been good to have known your birth parents at that time?"

Helen: "No. I would have thought of Mom [adoptive mother] as Mom and my natural mother as friend but I probably would have done a lot of things wrong when I was young. Now I'd be able to handle it. You know, and talk to her. When I was younger I would have wanted to go with her. And I'd have regretted it now."

And Judy, aged fourteen, who told me at one point that knowing about her birth parents would be good because she might want to go and live with them, answered the question, "How would you fit your birth parents into your life?" with a defensive, "I'd meet them, but I want to live with my [adoptive] parents. I'd treat my birth parents as friends but that's all."

I sat in homes, and coffee shops, and let this wave of feelings for adoptive parents wash over me in a surprising tide of positive emotion. I realized that you saw your *relationship* with your adoptive parents as important. You talked about it, reveled in it, argued with it, fought it and appreciated it. You felt surrounded by parental feeling, even saturated by it; but you still wanted to know where you came from, why you were given up and who your first parents were. You *knew* where you were; you wanted to know where you began.

Some of you have had bad experiences with parents, both birth parents and adoptive parents. Lori is eighteen although she looks much younger, is thin, has brown eyes and a cloud of mahogany hair waving to her shoulders. She was alone in her foster mother's house so she could tell me frankly about her experience with adoption.

When she was two years old her birth mother dropped her off at a friend's house and never came back. Her father looked for her and her brother and took them home to live with him for two years and then sent them to his parents. From there they were sent to a series of foster homes until Lori was seven. They were adopted and Lori lived with her adopted parents until she was fourteen. Her brother stayed with the adoptive parents only two years and then, because he wet the bed, they returned him to the social worker who placed him in a foster home. Lori had no idea that her brother was leaving until the social worker came to pick him up. The social worker had signed an agreement with her father that the two children would not be separated but her brother was taken away. Lori resented that at the time and still resents it.

A year after Lori was adopted into the family her adoptive parents had a baby girl. From then on, Lori felt her mother no longer wanted her. At eight years of age her mother used to punish her, Lori remembers, by making her write the same sentence five thousand times and by giving her many, many chores to do. I can't imagine a child writing something five thousand times (five hundred perhaps, but not five thousand). For every incomplete chore, her mother issued a punishment. It was a hard home life.

Lori would like to have a relationship with her sister now but her parents won't allow it. When she tried to phone her sister, her mother told her not to bother. Lori worries that her eleven-year old-sister is not safe because Lori had been sexually abused by her adoptive father from the time she was eleven until she left at fourteen. Good friends helped her as well as a perceptive and understanding social worker.

After Lori left her adoptive home she was placed in a foster home for eight months, then a group home for six weeks, and finally with the single parent foster mother she's been happy with for the last three years. She has "adopted" the children of this foster family as her brother and sister. Her natural brother disappeared from her life for years. He found his grandparents and lived with them and eventually contacted Lori; through him Lori found her father. He came to visit her last year and was not the man of her fantasies. He looked older than his years, had long, scraggly hair and a beard, was out of work, drank a lot and did drugs. Lori told me he was "disgusting."

Lori knows quite a lot about her birth mother. She was a hairdresser, lived in a northern city, is part Native Indian and was adopted herself. She knows her mother's married name, her maiden name and her alias but she hasn't met her. Lori would like to talk to her and ask her why she gave her up but she's not interested in any kind of a relationship with her birth mother or father.

Lori wants to be a legal secretary. She is sure that she can look after herself and be what she wants to be. She has little reason to think that anyone will help her.

8

YOUR FEELINGS ABOUT YOUR PLACE IN SOCIETY

Were you often reminded that you were adopted? Did your friends talk about it? Did the doctor ask you about it every time you had an appointment? Was it something that came up once a month or once a year? I didn't get specific answers but I did get replies to "Have you ever heard anything negative about adoption?" and, "Have you ever heard anything positive about adoption," as well as "Does 'being adopted' affect your life? Does it affect your future?"

If you are treated as a child with special status at home, it is sometimes a rude shock to find that the rest of the world doesn't care.

Some of you heard taunts from other six or seven year olds that strongly impressed you. "You're adopted. You aren't real." Small children, even when they have been told that they "were born in another lady's tummy," are often still shocked by the revelations of the playground. Children's attitudes toward adoption are often ones of great curiosity coupled with peculiar interpretations of their own. Years ago, when my oldest son was tiny, I had a state visit from a six-year-old neighbor.

"Mrs. Crook," she looked puzzled and avidly curious, "My mother says that your little boy is going to be a doctor. How can you know?"

I stirred that question around in my mind and finally said, "I think your mother said that my little boy is adopted."

Her face cleared. "That's it!" Then, "What's adopted? Isn't that some kind of doctor?" This little girl was always curious about relationships and feelings and went on to become a very good social worker.

The worst comments about adoption came from adoptive parents (in very few cases) and from junior high school friends and acquaintances who used the knowledge of your adoption as a mallet. You told me that no one else seemed to care.

Some of you weren't particularly sensitive to these taunts and suffered very little from them. I overheard a five-year-old girl tell her four-year-old brother, "Ha ha! You're adopted and I'm not!"

The mother leaned over casually and said, "And he has brown eyes and you have blue."

When I asked Barry how he reacted to teasing in junior high, he said he couldn't remember because he wasn't really interested in adoption at the time. But there are thirteen and fourteen year olds who are particularly sensitive. Debbie told me, "My older brothers always teased me. They used to bug me about it. 'Oh, yeah. You were the ugliest one there. Our parents felt sorry for you so they adopted you.' I used to hear things like that all the time. I believed it. I trusted my brothers. They were sometimes nice, and when they were, I just thought the world of them, at least until about last summer when I found out what kind of life they lead—drugs and alcohol. Really screwed up."

Joanne had no harassment from her family but she heard taunts from her "friends" in junior high school. "I'd hear, 'You were given up. You were ugly. No one wanted you.'" While Joanne understood that she was wanted by her family and that the teenagers were only looking for ways to be offensive, she was still hurt by the teasing.

Roberta, at nineteen, remembers the hurt she suffered when she was fourteen. "I remember being called a bastard. I remember kids at school saying, 'Those aren't your real mom and dad. That's not really your grandma and grandpa.' When they said that about my mom and dad I was almost afraid that they were right. But when they said that about my grandmother I *knew* they were wrong. My grandmother thought I was wonderful. And my grandmother was *mine.*"

"I remember the kids saying things like, 'Why would someone give their kid up for adoption?' 'Oh well, adopted kids have learning problems. They don't have the same feelings as everyone else.' I started to wonder if I was supposed to be normal! I couldn't talk to my mom and dad about it. I mean you lie so much to your parents when you're younger. You can't tell them how you feel. They have these expectations of the perfect daughter and you don't want to let them see any different. I had to grow up and they had to grow up and accept me."

Maryann felt that there was a lot of vulgar curiosity in the social world around her. "A lot of people feel you're not really a person. That's their attitude. They want to know how you deal with being given up." She naturally resented being questioned like this.

I hadn't realized that there was that much notice paid to the fact that you were adopted. I knew that many people have peculiar ideas about birth parents: that all birth mothers were all poor, unloved and ignored by their families; that birth fathers are uncaring. There is still the expectation, as Rhea said, "That I'd find my natural mother in the gutter." Many people, (adoptive parents, social workers, adopted children, and uninvolved observers) still feel that an unwed mother comes from an unfit family and lives in poverty. This attitude persists even in the people whose sister or an aunt or a neighbor placed a child for adoption.

John, in his prosaic and practical way, summed up the positive aspects. "Usually you're put up for adoption because your biological parents can't support you properly and they want something better for you. Your adoptive parents want you."

Leslie felt positive even though she was still arguing with her [adoptive] mother about her need to search. "I feel positive because I know a lot of kids who were adopted and didn't get along with their parents and couldn't handle the situation. They ended up going from foster home to foster home, or group home to group home, or group home to lock up. They ended up getting pregnant at fifteen and giving up a kid for adoption, somehow getting back at the whole process of adoption. So I feel good that I had a good home; I was lucky."

Judy, fourteen, viewed the parenting situation as a giant lottery–getting a good set of parents was purely a matter of luck. "Some parents are mean. If you search and find your natural parents you might not believe they really are yours and they might not live up to your ideas of them. The best thing about adoption and living with your adoptive parents is that you get a real family."

Helen had similar feelings about her family. "When you are adopted you can lead a normal life, a normal family life. Someone cared enough to put me out for adoption when they couldn't afford to keep me. They wanted me to have a good home. I've always seen adoption as a positive thing. I've never been mad at my birth parents for putting me up for adoption. I understand that a sixteen year old couldn't keep a baby–not really very well."

I don't want to leave the impression that people your age are constantly being questioned or put down by your peers. The incidents you described were isolated, but they impressed you. Generally you didn't find many people who gave your adoptive status much thought. When I asked if you thought that being adopted affected your lives, you told me that it didn't really make much difference to you and that it definitely wouldn't make any difference in your future. Even when it obviously had influenced some of you some during your junior high school years, you didn't expect it to make any difference to your adult lives.

Charlene's name and phone number were given to me by her older sister. Charlene was willing, but not eager, to talk to me. She was arranging the stock and financing for a men's accessory store but she agreed to make some time to see me. Clothing from her costume rental business was draped over furniture and the bed in her large, one-and-a-half room apartment on the top floor of a house in the suburbs. A guitar, a mandolin and a ukelele hung from pegs on the wall. She served me Grand Marnier coffee and then settled in an arm chair, sewing as she talked.

Charlene is an intelligent, poised, competent, nineteen-year-old and the possessor of an active sense of humor. I found the conversation slipping into off-the-record comments on men, sex, life in general and cabbage-patch dolls. Soft rock filtered down from the radio, mingling with the sunlight and the aroma of coffee, bathing us in comfort. Charlene herself provided the contrast to the atmosphere: sharp, astute. The youngest of two children, she keeps close contact with her parents, especially her (adoptive) mother but usually disagrees with her sister. She knew she was adopted at a very early age and was told quite a lot about her background including her name so she knows her past and isn't anxious about it.

The projects scattered around her apartment indicated that she is busy and active; she said she'd spun through project after project since she was seven years old when she had made the meals for her family, done the housework and involved herself in all kinds of school activities. Charlene is particularly close to her adoptive mother, rating her a ten plus. Her parents try to support her decisions and they helped her when she left home at seventeen to build a house and live in it with her boy friend. That didn't work out. Charlene went to college for a while and now supports herself with her sewing. She wants a home, husband and two children some day, and room on her property for her parents. But she's in no hurry. She's enjoying herself, her friends, and her life.

Charlene was interested in her sister's recent reunion with her birth mother. The reunion was important to her sister but it's not something Charlene wants for herself right now. While some day she *would* like to search and find her birth mother (Charlene feels she has a right to more medical history) she's not interested in a relationship. Charlene doesn't want to risk hurting her adoptive mother. Besides, she doesn't have time to search.

9

SEARCHING FOR YOUR BEGINNINGS

I met Barry in the city library where he had been spending the last two hours trying to track down a name in city directories. "Today's my day for Toronto and Saskatoon," he told me. "I have my mother's name but, since I was given up nineteen years ago, she probably married and changed her name, so I'm looking for her parents. I thought it would be easy but I'm having a hard time finding any information at all."

Barry is good-looking, personable, and athletic. He speaks easily and confidently, an asset in his jobs as a salesman in a sports shop in the winter and as a golf instructor in the summer. He lives in the suburbs with his adoptive parents and older brother and seems happy, stable, reasonable and intelligent. Although he had always known that he was adopted he hadn't been interested in it until this year. This year is his "year for searching." The local Parent Finders Association has helped him but he received no help from social workers. He sees this obstruction as a problem arising from the laws that instruct social workers to sacrifice his need in order to serve the interests of other people. He is sending letters to his elected representative trying to get some change in the law so searching will be easier for people like himself.

Barry and I ate our hamburgers and talked about the problems of searching for a past. He is curious and wants the information but he doesn't feel that his life would be blighted if he never finds it. His parents helped him get started, encourage him, and approve of his search. Barry has no plans to live with his birth parents or get very involved in their lives; but he'd like to sit down and talk to them as if they were friends he hadn't seen in a long time.

He had given his reasons for searching quite a lot of thought. "It took me three or four months to decide to search. I started by phoning the Zenith Child Line. She gave me the Parent Finders' number. So I phoned it one evening. I didn't know what was going to happen. I was really hopped up for it and I was kind of nervous. The phone answered, and it was a recording. It was the biggest let-down I'd had in the last little while. So then I sent off a letter and I got more and more interested. The head of Parent Finders here has given me a lot of advice. She isn't doing the search for me but she's giving me a lot of advice. I got hold of the lawyer who did the adoption and he still had my adoption order. He didn't want to give it to me at first but he finally did and that's how I found my name."

"I'm getting more and more interested in the search now. I asked the social workers for more non-identifying information and they wouldn't give me anything. To them it's not important. To me it is. I just want to know things like was my grandfather Ukrainian? It seems kind of stupid to be against the law to find that out. I know they're trying to protect the birth parents; they don't want anything coming back. I tried to get information from the hospital because technically, for a couple of days, *I* was a patient. The administrator said, 'Well, we can't give you information in case the mother doesn't want you to know. She could file a suit against us.' I'm not sure that I couldn't file one, too."

Because he works as a salesman Barry speaks persuasively. People would probably readily tell him information. "I'm really curious about my birth parents and my background. I think it will be interesting to know. What happens if I have an identical twin? I've thought about whether my girlfriend would turn out to be my sister [if she had been adopted too], or if my dad is a famous rock star. It's all really far-fetched but it's possible. I look at my best friend and I think, '*He* knows who his parents are. What gives the government the right to keep my background from me?' From reading my non-identifying background I get some reasons for what I am, why I happen to have a certain color of hair. And I play the piano. I took piano lessons for less than a year when I was twelve and I went through five books. It just seemed natural to me and it turned out that my birth father was a musician. He made his living playing in bands for a while."

Me: "How do you get people to give you information?"

"You have to tell stories because you can't go out and just tell people why you're looking. People might decide, 'Oh, this was all hush-hush way back then' and decide not to tell you anything. And then they might go and warn other relatives not to tell you anything. I make up a kind of story, say I'm looking for an uncle or something. I know enough from my non-identifying information to get some facts straight. What happens if I have a twin or a sister or something? I don't have a sister now, just a brother. Discovering a sister like that would be kind of interesting and neat. I think about that every once in a while. "

"I haven't put an ad in the paper yet. Every day I read the births, deaths, anniversaries, information wanted and some of the personals."

Some of you wanted to search for your birth fathers, but most wanted contact only with your birth mothers. I asked you why. The answers were much the same as what you wanted to know about yourselves. Your birth mother is your greatest source of information and you wanted to meet her to discover this information.

You also told me, "It would satisfy my curiosity." Lena said, "And give me a history. I'd just like to get to know her."

I was late for my appointment with Nicole at the fast food restaurant in the center of Vancouver. She was gone when I finally arrived. I called and she came back to meet me. Nicole is seventeen, a student in high school, the youngest of two children. Her older brother is not adopted.

By the time she was five, Nicole understood she was adopted. As she grew up she continued to be interested in adoption. She did a report on adoption for her law class in school and found, to her surprise, a negative attitude to adoption in the books she read.

Most of the books were written by authors who had been adopted after infancy and who wanted to return to their birth parents. Nicole didn't share their feelings at all. She knew why she had been given up for adoption and was satisfied that her birth parents did the reasonable thing. Her birth mother and father had been engaged but decided not to get married. One month later her birth mother found she was pregnant and chose to give Nicole to a two-parent family.

Nicole would like to meet her some day and get some medical history from her because she doesn't think the ("completely healthy") medical history she received is accurate.

Nicole is ambitious for her future, plans an academic career and told me that she was secure and happy where she was (she rated her parents nine out of ten). But, in spite of these feelings, she is still interested in knowing who she had been.

Nicole has mixed feelings about searching. "I wouldn't want to invade her [birth mother's] privacy. She might be living her own life, trying to block out what happened. It might have been a bad time in her life and I wouldn't want to bring it up again for her. I think I could accept that she might not want to see me. I don't think I would mind."

Sherry said that she too wanted to satisfy her curiosity. "I want to see what she looks like. I'm not looking for a new mother. My adoptive mother died four years ago, but I don't want a substitute."

Helen would like to know who her birth parents are. "To satisfy my curiosity about them. But it wouldn't bother me if I didn't find them. I'd like to find her [birth mother] but I'm not going to drop everything in my life to do it."

Karen feels a part of her [adoptive] family now that she is older, but she had a terrible time accepting herself when she was fifteen and sixteen. She still has problems with her status in society, and she wants to find and meet her birth mother. "If I met her it would be very scary. All I want to know is *why* she gave me up—the reason. And I want some medical history. A lot of times I get upset. I just want to know who she is. I have my world now. And I have this fantasy world out there with a mother in it. So what I'm living in my mind is two worlds, and before I can become settled with my life I have to bring those two together. "

"Ever since I was fifteen, I've wanted to meet her. Every woman I see of the right age, I wonder, is that my mother? Where do I fit in? My [adoptive] mother helped me try and find information. She really helped me. It's funny, but my brother and sister [both adopted] have no urge to find their birth parents. But my family knows how much it means to me to find mine. It means finding out more about me. My [adoptive] parents asked for more information when I was fifteen and they got it. But I still want to meet her and talk to her and find out *why* she gave me up."

Many of you want to see your birth mother, perhaps meet and talk to her, but are wary of getting involved. "She's a stranger, after all," Paul said. "What if I got myself tangled in this giant situation?"

Some of you aren't sure that you would actually want to meet your birth parents if you had more information about them. Even Karen said, "I say I'd like to meet her. It would satisfy my curiosity, give me a background and a medical history. I'm doing so much and I've put my [adoptive] mom through so much trying to get to meet her, but I might not want to do it once I got my file in front of me [the identifying information]. I'll decide whether I want to go any further then."

Dora felt that meeting her birth parents, both of them, would help "establish my identity. I look at people on the street and wonder. Knowing who my birth parents are would lay a ghost for me." But she is not looking for substitute parents. "I'm still in good contact with my foster mother. I introduce her as my mom. She's the one who accepts me as I am. Mothering is a feeling. It's a feeling of closeness, knowing that that person, that mother, is going to stand behind you no matter what."

According to Dora, that doesn't come with blood ties or with a piece of paper that makes you legally part of a family. It comes with learning to love someone and that can happen with no legal or biological ties at all. Dora's need to find her birth mother is not related to her need to have a mother. She clearly doesn't expect a stranger to mother her. What she needs from her birth mother is the information that will allow her to belong to the human family. She needs to know the biological facts of her beginnings –knowledge that can end her speculation.

Mike did not want to find his birth parents. "What if you knew them and if they were to find out you were that kid they put up for adoption? I don't know. I think you'd have lots of hurt feelings."

Many of you are concerned that searching for your birth parents will hurt your adoptive parents. You recognize the need in yourselves to have more information, perhaps even a meeting, but are reluctant to hurt the people you love. "My dad would be threatened," Sarah told me, "even though I feel that my mom and dad are the ones I have, not the ones who conceived me. My [adoptive] mom would help me, in fact, she did help me. She saved all the information. She even peeked at the adoption papers when the social worker left her alone in the room. She remembered the information, including my birth mother's name, and gave it to me when I was fifteen. I didn't tell Dad though. I don't think my mother told him either. He would be upset. So I have my birth mother's name and I looked it up in the telephone book. But I wouldn't phone her. That wouldn't be fair to her, don't you think? Maybe someday I'll get someone else, maybe a searching agency, to call her or find out if she wants to meet me. But not yet."

Many adoptive parents at the time a baby is placed with them receive some papers containing "non-identifying history." This is a description of the birth parents and often of their parents as well. It has been the policy of many agencies in many provinces and states to include racial origin, height of the parents, skin coloring, eye color, any talents, such as musical ability, and a medical history. This seems a cold picture to many of you–almost as if you were handed a parent from a record collection. Many of you don't have even this information. The problem may be that the adoptive parents didn't get it, or they got it and never passed it on to you, or it was never taken in the first place.

Roberta is fair, pretty, and really eager to talk to me about adoption. She lives with her parents and her seventeen and seven year-old brothers (neither are adopted). Roberta's family moved into this area, about an hour from Vancouver, when she was twelve. She had no friends at that time and felt unwanted. From being a good student at school and an easy-going child at home she became big trouble.

Roberta started to lie to her parents all the time. Not only did she shoplift, but she was the leader of a group and planned shoplifting forays into the stores of the town so that the gang would think she was smart, daring, "cool." She did some drugs, left school, got work, was fired from her job. Then she got pregnant and told the father of the baby. He denied responsibility so she told her parents she'd been raped. It seemed that nothing she did was helping.

One day she took everything she could find in the medicine chest at home and drank it. She was very sick (she said she had the worst case of diarrhea in her life) but she didn't hurt herself or the baby.

At fifteen she placed her baby boy for adoption. She wrote him a letter telling him why she placed him for adoption, and put her name in the reunion registry, making it as easy as possible for him to find her if he ever wants to; but she realizes that he may never want to.

Roberta told me about it. "I wrote him and told him why I had to give him up. I told him how much that I cared and I stayed in the hospital with him those ten days. I fed him and washed him and looked after him. For those ten days I was his mother. I'll always have that time with him and he had that time with me. *My* [birth] mother found me 'inconvenient.' She was thirty-one. See, there's no excuse. I was just inconvenient. I want to know how my birth mother felt. It's very, very hard to accept the fact that you were given up just because you didn't show up in time. You know 'Oh, well. Today's not convenient. We'll give you up today. If I'd had you a year from now, maybe I'd have kept you.' I find that hard." And yet that is what happened to Roberta. She had a baby at a time when she couldn't look after him.

"It would be nice to meet them [birth parents] and find that, 'Hey, they didn't really feel this way.' Maybe there's some *hidden* reason. I'd like to know what they look like. I fantasize so much. It's so easy to believe that maybe she's a frog or maybe she's a princess. And my father? I can picture him as very handsome in his uniform. Very good-looking, very easy-going. Maybe it's because the data I have now is so wonderful. "

"And her? I'd like to see what she looks like. It's kind of scary not knowing what you're going to look like when you get old. What if this woman, when she is sixty, looks like a real toad? It would be nice to know. It would be nice to know the medical part too. It would be nice to know a bit more about her personality. I mean they [social workers] said she was independent, responsible, hides her emotions, is likable and cooperative. Which can pretty well describe me; but there has to be more. I mean a person can't be described in eight words. It would just be so neat to meet them. I mean I'd never want her as a mother. I'd never want him as a father. But maybe just to answer questions.

"I hope *my* boy comes back to me. It would be nice to tell *him* some things. I have nothing to tell him except about me. There's nothing I can do about that. I have to find out my medical history before I can tell him what his is. I told him all I could about his background: about my four missing teeth–that's heredity–and all kinds of things he might want to know some day. I tried to give him a medical history but I don't have any past myself because *I* was never given one. There are good things too. It's nice to know that somebody cared enough about me to take me in. I feel special. I could have been one of those kids who was left for nobody and gone from foster home to foster home. It's nice to have roots.

"I think being adopted and giving a child up for adoption makes me more aware of how special it is to be adopted. You hear things. Sometimes I hear a story that kind of matches my own and I feel for that person. I really want to help them.

"I want to ask my birth mother questions. Somebody can put it on paper but it's so unemotional. Even if I walked up there and she said, 'Look, I didn't want you then; I don't want you now....'" Roberta's voice hardened with anger. "If she had the guts to tell me that, I'd believe her. Cruel or not, at least it's a dead-end answer which would be nice. It's so easy to build fantasies in your mind and, like I said, you think you might walk in the door and she'll embrace you, 'Oh, I love you! I'm sorry! I'm sorry!' It's so easy to pretend that way. It would be nice to know—really know. You might really let yourself in for a real bad knock-down if you fantasize like that, but it's hard not to do it. "

"If I'd met her at thirteen it would be different from now. Maybe I'd have been looking for another mother then. Like I could have had two moms then instead of one mom. Instead of now, when I would be looking maybe for a friend and some answers. Now I've got my mom and I don't need another one and I don't want another one either. "

"If I wanted to find her I guess I could put an ad in the paper. Sometimes I'll read an ad and it kind of hurts, I'll see an ad that talks about someone born the same year as me, the same month, wrong day. It's a boy not a girl and I think, is that ever nice but . . . why couldn't she do that for me? I got the pamphlets [from a searching organization] but they want so much money and I really don't have the money."

It's a good idea to write the searching organization you're interested in and ask what they will do for you and how much it will cost. Roberta was wrong. In her case, she could have registered in a reunion registry for no cost or the donation of a dollar or two and received advice and encouragement.

The barriers to finding out more information about birth parents and the barriers to actually contacting birth parents are, for the most part, the legal protection offered by the provincial and state laws to protect the identity of the birth parents. A great forest of laws seems to surround the birth parents keeping them secret, hidden, separate from those who want to know them. Less importance is given to the needs of the child than to the needs of the birth parents and the adoptive parents concerned that they be protected from harassment from the birth parents. Lawyers hired by the adoptive parents are hired to protect the concerns of their clients. Generally, adoptive parents ask for secrecy—no names, no identifying information. In most cases, parents think this is best for their child's future. They don't understand their child's need to know his original name. I didn't really understand that until you told me.

Lawyers do what they can to conscientiously assure that the

birth parents have no way of finding the adopted child. In many provinces and states there is a law which prevents both adopted children and adults from searching for and finding their own adoption order. In British Columbia, it is section fifteen of the Adoption Act: ". . . an adoption order is not subject to search. No person other than the Attorney General or a person authorized by him in writing, may have access to them; but the court, on an application"

This means that even adopted adults cannot search to find their birth name and birth parents. There are similar laws in other provinces and states. In some areas, these laws are made useless when adopting parents and birth parents exchange information before the adoption placement. After that, there is no need to search.

The need for protection of birth parents and adoptive parents isn't a scientific fact. It was a generally-approved social theory of twenty years ago. The purpose of the law was to help make the adoptive family more homogeneous. An adopted child was supposed to be absorbed into the family like the cream in a bottle of homogenized milk. Shake up the family and let there be no differences between adopted and natural children.

Opinions and attitudes have changed over the years. Adoptive parents and birth parents feel the need to be more open with one another. More and more adoptions now involve a meeting of both sets of parents before the child is placed. If the meeting occurs privately it is not subject to any provincial or state regulations. In most instances, the agency cannot arrange such a meeting but it is willing to cooperate after the meeting has taken place. Perhaps the next generation of adopted children won't worry about their origins; they'll know who they are.

You tell me that you feel closer to your adoptive families when your parents help you explore your background, when parents encourage you to be yourself, when your parents recognize that you are unique, different from them. The old adoption laws underlined the idea that you didn't exist before the adoption order. If as a teenager or adult you cling to reality, and insist that you *are* an individual and you *did* exist before adoption, you may be considered emotionally unstable.

In one sense, this attitude of lawmakers, social workers, and many adoptive parents is wonderful. They are concerned that you be given every chance to be truly a child of your new family. But you don't see any need for great secrecy. When asked if you received any different treatment or if being adopted affects your lives socially, not one found any prejudice—except in junior high school. Being adopted today is not a social problem. Twenty years ago adoption was not so readily accepted.

If all people, every human on earth, had no knowledge of their biological beginnings, you probably wouldn't worry about it either. How would families operate if everyone—your parents, your grandparents—was adopted and no one had any history?

Some of you feel that you have been invited to a party holding a different color invitation from everyone else; that you are only a temporary guest; that you might be asked to leave at any moment. This feeling of difference, this lack of background information, instead of uniting families, as the lawmakers and social workers once predicted, is causing problems within families. In cases where your adoptive parents help you find information, you tell me you feel closer to your parents. When helped to find your beginnings you feel understood, loved and appreciated. You feel your individuality is respected and accepted.

There is no question that many of you feel the need to search. As Barry said, "I didn't talk about it to many people. I didn't think it was important to anyone else. But I want to know about my background so I'm doing my own search. When you decide that you're going to search you have to be prepared to live with whatever you find. If you aren't ready to accept what you find, I don't think you should bother to search. You will have to accept the good or the bad whichever way it turns out to be. After I find them I don't intend to change. I'm happy. I'm satisfied. I just want to know who they are."

10

INVESTIGATING
YOUR HISTORY

Few of you actually know the name of your birth parents. I met four. In some provinces and states the names of the birth parents are given to the adoptive parents at the time of placement; in some areas the name used to be given to the adoptive parents but now is held back. Most of you start with little or no information so it takes ingenuity and persistence to trace your past. It's not easy and it takes time.

All provinces except Quebec, Prince Edward Island, Newfoundland and the Northwest Territories have some kind of provincial registry. Usually they accept registration from adult adoptees and birth mothers. Some provinces charge a fee for their services. Some provinces have a backlog of work so that they will not attempt to help you for two years.

The registries differ from state to state, from province to province. Some are passive registries in which both the birth parents and the adoptee must register and are then "matched." Some registries are active in which case, either the birth relatives or the adoptee may ask for the agency to search for the other party. Some are "semi-active," in which case, only the adult adoptee is helped in a search. The birth relatives will not be assisted. Some registries have so many applications for searches and so few staff members that they are seven to ten years behind in their work.

In Ohio and Colorado such a registry exists in the Department of Health but you must be twenty-one before your request is processed. Similar registries exist in South Dakota, Kansas and Arkansas. Countries such as Scotland, England, Wales, Israel and Finland allow free access to the records by adopted adults. Now that the records are available in England only a small percentage of adopted adults actually look up their backgrounds. It seems that when the information is easy to get many people don't try to look.

Laws change and you might find, by the time you read this book, that your province or state has changed its laws and information is now easier to obtain.

There are many private registries that serve the adopted adult's need to find information. They offer advice, and moral support and suggest searching techniques. Some of their addresses appear in Appendix I of this book. The Canadian Reunion Registry accepts names from all who wish to search. Again, you must be eighteen or your adoptive parents must act for you. Send your name, address, birth date, birth place and time of the day you were born. They fill out a card and keep it on file waiting for your birth parent to offer the same information. The Reunion Registry ties into the American International Soundex Reunion Registry which accepts searchers at eighteen years of age.

The Canadian Adoptee's Reform Association also has a reunion registry and there are, as well, other private registries started by interested searchers. They will often accept your information, put it in a holding file and ask you to wait until you reach eighteen. At the same time, they will give you advice and help. If you don't feel comfortable with the agency you first call, phone another one. Don't give up after one try. If your adoptive parents apply on your behalf some agencies will start a search.

There are several magazines devoted to the problems created by our social restrictions on adopted adults. *People Finders*, published in Batavia, Illinois, USA, lists many searching agencies; some of them volunteer, non-profit organizations and some of them private, detective-like inquiry agents. In the August 1985 issue of *People Finders* I counted fifty-four agencies listed for the state of California. That's a little overwhelming. How do you know which agency to pick? Just look over what's available to you and pick one. If you don't like it, try again.

The first place to start searching is at home. If you can, talk to your (adoptive) parents. They are your best source of information for they often recall facts that are important leads in your search. They may remember bits of information the social worker gave them many years ago. They may have a letter or a report filed away. Cooperative adoptive parents can be a great source of support and help and the process of looking for your birth parents can draw you and your adoptive parents closer together. Spend time with your parents explaining and persuading them to help you. Often parents can find information quickly and, in some states and provinces, adopted children, even adult adopted children, need their parents' consent to obtain information. There will be instances when even great efforts won't produce the name of your birth relatives. No one can promise you success here. They can only try.

Leslie started looking for her birth mother when she was nineteen. "For me, it was hard because my parents were not supportive. My mother is very insecure. But she should have been a little more secure to know that, after nineteen years of her being my mother, I wasn't going to run off with someone who was . . . like a perfect stranger. She *should* have been supportive, but fear overcomes love there, because they [my parents] were more afraid that I was going to find them [my birth parents] and want to go back there. I don't know why, but I suppose if I was a parent I would have that attitude too. "

"I couldn't talk to my mother because she got very upset . . . to the point she would phone me and somehow we would get into it and she would cry on the phone. All I wanted to do was know. And I'd gotten mad at her a few times because it had got to the point that it annoyed me that she would be that insecure. You're my mother. You're my father. That's all there is to it. It's just that I want to know who they [birth parent] are; why they gave me away; what the circumstances were. My mom just had a really hard time handling it. Parents are better off supporting the child and helping her through it. Like a child is better off if she goes somewhere to meet her [birth] mother and her mother tells her, 'Well, I got pregnant and I was a hooker and I didn't want you.' Then you're better off to have your [adoptive] mother there to cry on."

If you have decided to search for your background, and you know your birth name try to find information the following ways. (This information was obtained from the secretary of the Canadian Reunion Registry.)

1. Check telephone directories (old telephone books in library "stacks"). Look for a father or brother of your birth mother. Male relatives are less likely to change their last name.

2. Check city directories showing residence, occupation and full name. Main branches of libraries and archives keep directories going back to 1900. Check others at the same address in the back and note names of neighbors for possible contact. Some museums keep genealogy lists.

3. Try to trace your birth parents through their past. Look for obituaries that name nearest relatives such as, "Mr John Smith is survived by his daughter Rose." Obtain a copy of your grandparents death certificates from Vital Statistics, and a copy of all papers filed with a probate from Surrogate Court. In some provinces, this is called Probate Registry to the Supreme Court. In your state you can get your ancestors' names from the State Department of Vital Statistics. This will tell you in what county your ancestor died. Then apply to the County Superior Court for information on Probate.

4. Write to Public Archives, Genealogy Division, 395 Wellington St., Ottawa Ontario. In the U.S., write to Genealogy Department of the Church of Jesus Christ of Latter Day Saints, 50 East N. Temple, Salt Lake City, Utah, 84150.

5. Look for church marriage records.

6. Try the voters lists kept at city hall if there are any.

7. Check automobile registrations if that is possible in your province or state.

8. Talk to bill collectors.

9. Try relatives no matter how distant.

10. If you find a document, try talking to all people whose names appear on the document including witnesses or an attending priest or minister.

11. Search for employers your birth parents may have had.

12. If they were in a unionized-type of employment, have the

union check their records. If they graduated from high school or university check their school records. They may give you some idea of their former address. You may even find a picture.

13. Hospital records. In some provinces, it is the law for a hospital to keep a record of all births until the child reaches the age of majority. Providing the file has not been added to, the hospital may then destroy these records.

14. Check the newspaper: information wanted, missing persons, personal, anniversary, obituaries, marriages.

15. Check old newspapers for marriages, births or deaths.

16. Persevere.

If you don't have your birth name, but do have non-identifying information, search through the information for anything that can be traced. You act like a detective, a bill collector, a tax collector. You snoop, and question and even lie a little. You need to look for any indication of what high school your birth parents attended, any awards they might have won in what year, any kind of employment they or their parents had that might have left a record. Social workers sometimes get tired of blocking out the names in the non-identifying information report so, near the end of the report, look for a partially rubbed-out name and try to put it together with pieces from another partially rubbed-out name.

Some people take this search as an intense emotional journey and some take it as an intellectual challenge. "With the odds against me, the world against me, I'll win," Barry said. "It's like my theme song is 'Never Surrender'."

Rhea found her birth mother by putting together all the information she could, and, at seventeen, searching by herself. "I knew she had been a teacher, that she was blonde, five-foot-six inches, blue eyes. I didn't know where she lived but I knew she had grade thirteen in Ontario. I had my last name narrowed down to five names. I found that out by snatching glances at the records as the social workers pulled them out."

Leslie told me of her search. "The name of the town my birth mother lived in was on the adoption form. I figured it was a small town and there must be somebody there who knew what was going on. I wrote to the church. The minister might know. He might tell me a lot about her without telling me her name. I didn't have to know who she was. I just needed to know more about her. I thought so, anyway. I wrote to the Children's Aid Society there. They've got two Children's Aids' there. I wrote to the hospital and I wrote to the library checking for birth announcements from that date [Leslie's birthday].

"And what happened was that the lady in the library knew the family, knew that there was another child out there, and she forwarded my letter to one of my sisters who still lived out there. And my sister answered the letter not letting on for a minute that she knew who I was or that she knew that she was my sister. She just asked me what I wanted to know and I wrote back and told her. I didn't care if they had a million bucks. All I wanted was to know. I wasn't in it for the money.

"And the hospital made the mistake of writing back and telling me. They aren't supposed to disclose that kind of information but they wrote back and they told me that there was a child born to Mary Smith and she named me the same name as she had. She named me after herself. And they made the mistake of telling me. Maybe they didn't realize what they were doing. Or maybe she [birth mother] put it in there that if anyone ever did inquire they were allowed to give out the information. But I was under the impression that they weren't.

"The only way I can find out who my father is is to go and see my mother. And my sisters tell me that she's not ready for that. They knew my mother had me because they were all seventeen or eighteen at that time. And they knew that I would come back some day and find them. My sisters were worried that I would tell my [birth] mother and her husband. But I didn't want to do that. It doesn't matter that I'm not going to meet her. The only reason I would like to meet her is to know who my father was. He's not her husband. I don't want to upset her life.

"When I decided to search I took for granted what I didn't know and I figured the best way to search was very, very slowly and very, very quietly so as not to attract a whole bunch of attention. I've met my sisters but I don't have much to do with them. They've got their lives and I've got my life. I don't know if I'd want a relationship with my [birth] mother if I did meet her. I don't know about that."

When you decide that you want to search for your birth parents how can you be sure that you will receive information and not an unexpected and unwanted visit from your birth mother or father? Well, you can't be one hundred percent sure. It is the policy of searching agencies not to allow unscheduled meetings between searching parties. You are supposed to be asked if you want a meeting. But occasionally mistakes are made and a birth mother bypasses an agency and makes direct contact. This is rare, but it can happen. And it has happened.

Joining a searching group can give you a sense of acceptance. The others in the group can help you accept your needs as reasonable and normal. Since they are experienced searchers they can give you advice and help. Most organizations will not actively assist you in searching for your birth parents but they will provide information and advice on how to deal with the problems you do have. As you have probably already realized, people who are adopted differ widely in their acceptance of themselves. Some people have a curiosity that needs limited information to satisfy. Some people have an almost obsessive need to understand their birth parents and they want a great deal of information.

Each one of you has to decide what it is you must discover and how important it is to you. Many of you at about fifteen or sixteen are working through feelings of independence and have difficulty with your adoptive parents (particularly your mother). At times you think that all your problems would be solved if you could only meet your birth parents. You could be magically freed from the task of "working things out" with your (adoptive) parents. You would be loved and understood with an instinctive acceptance by "real" parents.

There aren't any magical ways of working out a relationship. It takes time and effort. Everyone works at this problem, adopted or not. Dealing with relationships, solving the problem of loving and loving authority, are usual tasks of teen life. This must not be confused with searching for your original history. Teens who are not adopted often "adopt" another set of parents during this turbulent time. They tell their own parents nothing and tell their friends' parents everything. I've often wondered if it wouldn't be wise to "trade" fifteen-year-olds around the neighborhood. You'd go to the neighbor's and her kid would come to live at your house. Some of you told me that you stayed with aunts or neighbors for a while when you were sixteen, so perhaps this is already happening!

Most searching agencies understand this painful growing period and will advise you to wait until you are eighteen. By then, you have resolved most of your problems of independence, and some of the problems of identity, and are ready and strong enough to take on new relationships.

Debbie told me very firmly, "I'm sixteen. I have a set of parents [adoptive]. I have foster parents, a sister and two brothers. I have a foster sister and brother, a boy friend, school and a job. I don't have *time* for any more relationships."

While a group of searchers can be a great support to you, the members of the group are not your prototypes. There are no clones here. No one will be exactly the same as you; no one will have your identical problems. You'll find people with different ideas and different needs. But you will find information and understanding.

Not all of you want to search for your beginnings. Some of you just want to talk to someone about it, want to work out your feelings, get your ideas clear. You can talk to professional counselors: school counselors, ministers, social workers. Or you can find a friendly aunt or uncle, an older brother or sister. Sometimes you can find a neighbor who is easy to talk to, listens well and gives good advice. Perhaps all you want to do about the curiosity you have about your past is talk about it.

11

YOUR LEGAL STATUS

Birth parents give up their right to their child and can't, on some future day claim the child. Mike at fifteen had not known this.

Mike "They gave me up. That's done. They don't have the right to take me back, do they?"

Me: "No, they don't."

Mike: "Are you sure?"

Me: "Yes, I'm sure."

Mike: (with relief) "That's good."

The Adoption Act is a provincial act in Canada and a state act in the U.S. These acts establish that you are a legal child of the family, a status that is binding everywhere.The law removes any legal differences between natural children and adopted children. You are, legally, the same. You can expect the same rights and privileges as a natural child and can inherit equally with natural children. The acts result in the same legal status for all children but they differ from province to province and state to state in the way the records are available for searching.

The adoption process is not simple and straightforward in all parts of the country. Each province or state has its own rules, policies and practices. It's been a practice of some religious and political organizations to have their own adoption agencies so they can place the children of their members within their own group. "Burden Bearers," a private placement agency, operates in Canada and the U.S. placing children in "Christian" homes, that is homes that meet the religious requirements of the agency.

"Jewels for Jesus Adoption Agency" is another agency whose main concern is to place children in homes approved by this particular group, adding more souls to their religious community. "Latter Day Saints Social Services," "Families for Children (international adoptions only)," "Advocate Adoption Services" and "Catholic Family Services" are some of the private agencies in North America. Native Indian organizations are also interested in placing children of Native Indians with their own families. The majority white population also mostly demands white babies for white homes. Some black organizations in the United States have a similar philosophy.

In private adoptions, the child is usually in the home when the visit is made and the welfare worker would have to have grounds for apprehension in order to remove the child. In spite of some bad publicity, private adoptions are not necessarily poor adoptions. Adoption, after all, began as private adoption. Large private systems, such as Catholic Charities, have been placing children in good homes for years. Children adopted by aunts and uncles, by step-fathers and step-mothers and by neighbors are usually adopted privately.

All the above organizations are interested in furthering the advancement of their ideas by absorbing the children. In most cases, attention is paid to the needs of the child but the prime concern of these organizations is to add more people to their group. They have ideals and policies that can be made stronger by indoctrinating children to their way of life. The motivation of the adopting parents may be, even in these placements, loving and accepting. The parents who adopt don't necessarily reflect the ideals of the placement agency, although they are chosen because the agency thinks they do. Sometimes parents agree to the organization's policies in order to adopt a child.

Once the child is legally part of their family, the parents may not follow the policies set up by the adopting organization. In many cases, the needs of the children have been neglected by the provincial or state adoption agencies. Children born of minority races historically have been placed in foster homes rather than adopted. Almost any new placement agency would be better than the ones some groups have had to use. Native Indian babies had a particular problem because, for many years, little effort was made to place them in homes in their communities. They were considered "hard to place" but neither the adoption agencies nor the Indian communities themselves set up any system that would assure a stable home for every child. Now, the Indian communities in many areas are actively sponsoring welfare programs that give attention to the needs of such children.

The philosophy of government agencies now is to serve the best interests of the child, the birth mother, and then the interests of the adopting parents. While that is the philosophy, in practice some government workers are incompetent and/or overwhelmed with work. If the best interests of the child are to be served, then the child would most often be placed in a family that already has children, has been proven stable and has years of practice at raising children. As it seems much fairer to the adopting parents to place children in families with no children or with only one child, and as such families are in a position to complain about the service they aren't getting from the agency, the practice of most agencies is to place a child with childless couples (or with couples with one child) first.

Social workers may appear to shuffle adoptive homes in what seems to you to be a capricious game of chance in judging the needs of the child and the needs of parents, with estimates of how long they think the marriage of the adoptive parents is going to last. The lucky winner gets a baby. In fact, there is a system in most agencies of careful matching. Adopting parents are selected by the social worker and birth mother to match, as closely as possible, the religious, academic and socio-cultural background of the birth mother. One knowledgeable and experienced social worker told me that the most successful matches occur when the birth mother thinks the description of the adopting parents sounds like a description of her family.

Kendra, now twenty years old, gave a child up for adoption four years ago. "The social worker told me that if I wanted to keep my baby I'd have to do it on my own; that welfare wouldn't help me. She told me it was illegal for me to get welfare and to hurry up and decide."

In fact, the policy of the welfare department of her province was to support the mother if she wanted to keep the child. Kendra had very bad luck in her choice of social worker.

"I couldn't make a quick decision. I wanted to look over the files of adopting homes really carefully; so I put my baby in foster care for two weeks while I read the files and tried to decide. The social worker told me to hurry; that they had a problem getting homes and that I had to pick one of the four she offered me. I insisted on seeing more files. The social worker told me that my baby was screaming all the time and I had to hurry to get her into a good home. I was totally honest with the social worker and she lied to me. I have a real grudge against social workers now. I never saw that worker again after she placed my baby. I wanted to be left alone when I was pregnant and no one would leave me alone. And then after, when I needed someone, they all left me alone."

"I wanted to write a letter to the parents when my baby was six months old but the social worker said they didn't want to hear from me, so to 'forget it.' She hung up the phone on me."

"The social worker would do things like keep me waiting in the office. I'd have a one p.m. appointment and she would be across the street eating lunch; I could *see* her and she'd keep me waiting until two. She treated me that way, maybe, to make me feel inadequate so I'd give up the baby easier. My social worker specialized in adoption."

"The father of the baby offered to help me. He offered me money and he offered to marry me. But a kid is no basis for marriage, so I didn't want that. And my mother was strange. She and my father were divorced and she had some funny ideas. I was afraid that she'd charge the father of my baby with rape because I was only sixteen, so I wouldn't tell anyone who he was. I thought my mother could have had him sent to jail. I wish I'd had some legal advice."

Kendra's baby had a choice of adoptive homes because the number of babies available for adoption is far less than the number of waiting couples. Women and men are more careful about birth control now than they were in the past. Birth control is easier and more available so there are fewer unplanned pregnancies. If a woman has some support from her parents, from her boyfriend or her grandparents, she is more likely to keep her child now than she was in the past. And while legal abortion is an option today, effective birth control is still the most significant reason why fewer babies are available for adoption.

The strongest check on all social agencies regarding the placement of the baby is the demands of the birth mother. If she demands that a certain order of priority be followed in placing her child, her child is more likely to achieve a good home. But most birth mothers, like Kendra, are young and emotionally vulnerable right after their delivery. It's hard to be strong when you are physically tired from childbirth and emotionally distressed at parting with your child. Some birth mothers have parents who harass them. It's hard, right after childbirth, to make demands of the social workers.

Occasionally, the birth mother has not signed a release and her child can't be placed for a legal adoption. In these cases, a child may go to foster care and then sometimes be forgotten in the bureaucracy of the welfare office. Some agencies such as the Department of Human Resources in British Columbia have a system of "tracking" in place which now should prevent children from "disappearing between papers" in the welfare office. There is no system of legal checks and balances that forces any social worker to do his best to find a child an adoptive home. That is a moral and professional obligation felt strongly by most social workers.

My family had wonderful social workers when we were looking for our sons. We had competent, caring workers with a sense of humor. I had worked with many social workers when I was a public health nurse and had met a few who were less than competent, but only one that was uncaring. The stories you told me came as a shock.

Children who are given a status number (in Canada) as a native Indian are in the position of having the Indian Act (federal) take precedence over the Adoption Act (provincial). In the U.S., Indian children are not given a status number, they are enrolled in a tribe either with land under a treaty or without land. What they gain by being registered as Indian under the Indian Act can't be taken away by the Adoption Act. In these cases, the children are legally adopted but still have status as native Indians. This means that they have not only the rights of a legal child in their family but also the rights of a native Indian in Canada or the U.S.

In Canada, they have the right to apply to the tribal band in which they were registered for funds for post secondary education. They can also apply to live on a reserve and ask the band for any reasonable help with their lives. They can, at age twenty-one, choose to be a part of the band or choose to take a financial settlement from the band. The band could vote not to give such a settlement to the child but it is unlikely.

Occasionally, a band may decide that a child born of a band member but not registered as a status Indian may have the right to band funds. In the U.S., native Indian children have the right to the benefits of treaty if they are enrolled with a tribe that has treaty benefits, as well as having rights to health benefits, education and welfare. If they are without a treaty, they have the rights to health, education and welfare only.

If you are adopted and are also a native Indian, you must decide whether your native ancestry is a culture you wish to adopt or simply a racial origin you wish to absorb into your life the way other Canadians absorb their background a generation removed from Norway, Scotland or Italy. Many native groups feel that Indian people should control the destiny of Indian people. Such groups make the assumption that any native person, regardless of his history, retains his culture, whether that culture is the matriarchal one of the West Coast which the child's family may not have experienced for three generations, or the Cree way of life in Alberta that he remembers.

All make the connection between racial, physical characteristics and inherited cultural memory which, however unsupported, many believe to be true. Such a belief forms the basis of interest in children that have been adopted or placed in foster care away from the tribe. It is quite true that our welfare system has discriminated against Indian children, not placing them in permanent homes and causing hardship and heartbreak. Even if you don't agree with the motivation of groups that judge a child's best interest by his skin color, the placement by such groups may be of benefit to more children than the welfare system has been in the past.

None of you concerned yourself with the feelings of groups of adults motivated religiously or politically about adoption. You don't see yourself as saviors of religion or race and don't see why you should involve yourself with anyone else's problems with adoption.

Karen said, "To an adopted child, adoption is personal. People who are not adopted . . . should not speak about it or judge it." While no questions were asked specifically about race, some of you were in a mixed racial situation. You felt that race as well as adoption was a private affair. The Caucasian sister of a native Indian teenager told me about the racial differences between her and her brother, "It never occurred to me until one day I was introducing my brother to someone and I suddenly thought that they might think it odd that we had different colored skin. Until that time I'd never thought about it. He was just that color. Like I had blue eyes and he had brown. I was eighteen before I really noticed we were different."

Adoption often serves the best interests of the adoptive parents and the best interest of the adopting agency. Over the years, many people have been concerned about the child's best interests, but concerned people make decisions with the knowledge they have at the time and, very often, the best interests of the child are not clear. Amendments to the laws on adoption can be passed at any time. What seems to be written in blood one week can be changed the next. Lawmakers are responsive to lobbying by interested groups. You might want to write your member of the provincial or state legislature about what you want done to make the laws better for you. If you want to change what social workers do, you'll have to change the law. The social workers must operate under the law. They can't give you information if the law forbids it.

There are some incidences of babies being placed for private adoption in a system that seems to be buying and selling. Those incidences are confined to a few lawyers. Some provinces and states attempt to control this with laws such as the one introduced in 1980 in British Columbia whereby the law attempted to "prohibit the offering or accepting of a consideration of value in money or in kind for the purposes of inducing a person to make a child available."

The law was tested in 1982 when a couple applied to the Supreme Court to allow them to pay the birth mother of their child some recompense for her expenses. The judge allowed the adopting parents to pay the travel, medical and legal expenses of the mother. The courts don't want to make recompense for medical and legal expenses unavailable to the birth mother; they only want to try to prevent the birth mother from benefiting financially from the transaction–from creating a baby business.

The Law Societies of most provinces and states frown on lawyers charging exorbitant fees for finding a baby for a client. The lawyer is supposed to arrange the legal adoption, not be a broker for the clients. Lawyers' professional ethics should prevent baby brokering. You can report any lawyer you suspect of selling babies to his Law Society.

Some children are brought from foreign countries for adoption in the United States and Canada. But all children who are adopted in the U.S. and Canada must be adopted under the state and provincial laws. All children who are legally adopted have the same legal rights in their adoptive family. It makes no difference to the adoption order where you came from as long as the order is processed and passed. You become the adopted child of that family. An adoption order in one state or province is legal anywhere.

12

YOUR PROBLEMS
WITH SOCIAL WORKERS

Since most of you were critical of social workers, I called social workers across the country and asked them what they were doing out there. What was causing so much hostility? I knew that retaining birth information seemed to be the main frustration, so I asked workers in agencies from coast to coast about their policies and the rationale behind them.

I found social workers in the planning departments of provincial ministries desperately anxious to be effective, compassionate and to act in the "best interest of the child." I was impressed (and pleased) to find that the workers I talked to were intelligent, competent and very caring. For the most part, they were supervisors of family services and probably not the workers you would meet in the office. However, they were responsible for your worker and, in many cases, interpreted the policies to the social workers in the local offices.

They were surrounded by legislation, public opinion and individual lobbying which made it difficult for any one social worker to respond with simple, compassionate solutions. It isn't possible to give you information if the legislature and policies of the government forbid it.

In some cases, it is just as frustrating for the social worker to be prevented from acting in a simple, reasonable way as it is for you to be denied your background. As with all laws, the ones that cause you an injustice are unfair, and anyone who obeys such unfair laws seems to be colluding with injustice. Social workers are aware of this attitude. Their alternative is to ignore the law, betray their employer and leave themselves open for law suits and breach of trust actions. It is not much of a choice.

Many of you had a poor opinion of the social welfare system. Dora said, "I don't trust social welfare. How many kids can't see opportunities out there? Social workers don't help. If my child had to go through what I did, I couldn't handle the guilt."

Rhea's birth mother told her, "I made a contract with social welfare to place you in a good home. When it didn't work out, why didn't they get in touch with me? They broke their contract. Why didn't they come back and ask me if I could help you?"

Many of you feel that, while the system provides a good chance at a good home for you, it avoids telling you the truth and enters into a great conspiracy of information suppression and ignores the needs of the birth mother. Rhea didn't see why the birth mother couldn't have a periodic progress report from the adoptive parents on how her child was doing.

Dora was sure that a letter from the adoptive parents, given to social welfare and passed on to the birth mother, had a good chance of never arriving.

Sarah felt that she had a responsibility to let her birth mother know she was okay. "I'd like to tell her thanks and give her a hug."

Although many of you felt your birth mothers had a right to information about your well-being, you didn't feel your birth mothers had any right to interfere in your lives. Nor did you feel that the birth mothers had a right to contact you. You wanted the choice of meeting birth parents or not meeting them to be your decision. The Reunion Registry of Canada gives statistics on those who are seeking information about adoption. Seventy-five percent are adopted children seeking information and only twenty-five percent are birth parents. So while you see birth parents as having the right to knowledge about you, large numbers of them aren't asking.

You told me that the adoption-welfare system is "lousy". In some cases, this is a resentment of a social and legal system that controls information that you want about your history. And, in some cases, this is an attitude that is the result of experience.

"The social worker put me in twelve foster homes before I was eight months old. I mean, what kind of a social worker would do that?" When I asked why she had so many homes Karen said, "I don't know. You wouldn't get a straight answer from a social worker. Social workers are government. They say anything to cover themselves up."

It's usual to blame the system when you are frustrated with the laws.

Dora said, "I don't trust the welfare. The way welfare works you have a one in thirty chance of turning out okay if they're looking after you." Although Dora had some good experiences with social workers, her most recent experience had not been happy.

Bill is twenty-two years old and has had a lifetime of frustration with social workers. We met over lunch and spent an hour talking about his life. I listened to his tape later trying to decide if he was acting or if he had truly lived through all the things he told me.

He is about five-feet ten-inches, dark, quiet, almost shy. He told me he had never talked to anyone the way he was talking this day. I thought he might perhaps be Native Indian, or perhaps part Chinese. He didn't know. His ignorance of his racial history is part of his problem.

Bill was in six or eight foster homes before he was six years old, then in an orphanage (he thinks). (It is more likely to have been a group home than an orphanage.) At age eight he was placed for adoption. Apprehended by the court at twelve, he then lived in several different group homes until he was nineteen. His adoptive parents have no history on him. The social workers say they gave his history to his adoptive parents and now don't have any records on him. This is unusual, because copies are usually kept in the welfare office. Bill isn't sure where he was born, or whether he is Canadian or American.

Although he was only with his adoptive parents for four years, he speaks of them as if they were his parents and of his adoptive brother and sisters as if they were his siblings. But he has no ties but legal ties to his adoptive parents, and few to his brother and sisters. He would like to search out his birth parents, not so much to establish a relationship, as to establish a solid background for himself. He seems afraid to develop any kind of relationship with anyone because he has suffered so much rejection. This fear is a problem—he knows that—but he doesn't know how to handle it.

Bill got good training as a cook and now works in a restaurant and has ambitions to work in an even better restaurant. He has another ambition; some day, he would like to know who he is.

"I remember meeting my [adoptive] parents, when I was about eight, at the fountain. It must have been Vancouver because I remember the Planetarium. I was apprehended by welfare when I was twelve. I remember going to court and sitting there from nine in the morning until two in the afternoon. No one told me what was going on. No one told me what was happening. They just told me to be quiet and do as they said. They did tell me that my parents were charging me with 'unmanageability.'"

"I knew I hadn't done anything wrong. But the social worker told me to keep quiet and just not say anything so they could get me out of that home. She said if I tried to tell anyone that I hadn't done anything, they'd put me back with my parents, and I didn't want that. [As a legal child of his adoptive parents Bill could not be simply returned to the social worker. He had to be apprehended or taken in custody as a delinquent.]"

"I talked to my best friend later. His father, a policeman, thought my parents were treating me so bad he reported them to welfare and that's why the welfare tried to help me. When I was older, I tried to get my background information and the social workers said they didn't have it. They have no records of me before I was eight. So they said. It's like it's okay with them; I didn't exist until I was eight. "

"They put me in a couple of group homes and they were okay, but I always knew I was leaving a place on the day I had to go. Always on the day. I never had any warning. And they never did any follow-up. I saw my social workers once in the first year I was away from my parents. And then no social worker for three years. Any help I got, I got from the secretaries at the welfare office. Not from any social worker. No one talked to me. No one cared. "

"No one cared until I got [into] a good group home. I had a

really good group home from when I was fifteen to when I was nineteen–just great. Except for those group home parents, the social system has left me in a bad situation. I'm supposed to have dual citizenship because I was born in the States. I've lived in Canada since I was eight but, because my parents won't give me any information and because the social workers say they don't have any, I can't get Canadian citizenship. I've been here since I was at least eight! It's like I didn't really exist. I had the R.C.M.P. try to find out information and the Canadian Armed Forces try (I'm in the Reserve. They wouldn't let me into the active service because I couldn't prove my citizenship) but they just get a blank before I was eight."

[I did check with a lawyer who was in the Armed Forces Reserve. He told me that any qualifications that were sufficient to get a person into the Reserve would also be sufficient to allow him into the active service.]

"Everyone's pretending that before I was adopted at age eight, I just wasn't anywhere. I've tried to find out but I got no help from any social worker. No one gave a damn and that's the truth."

It's maddening to think, like Bill, that information you want may be sitting in a file and a social worker won't give it to you. It doesn't seem important that he or she *can't* give it to you because the laws won't allow it. There is a danger that in blaming the social workers exclusively for your problem you will then not do anything else. You might feel that you are "doing something" by complaining when you could be trying to change the laws.

Some social workers have ethical problems when you ask for information. They usually understand your need to know but have difficulty justifying the release of information and reconciling the conflicting loyalties to their agency and past commitments of the agency. "We made a contract with birth parents and adopting parents eighteen years ago," one social worker told me. "We promised at that time not to reveal any identifying information. If we reveal the names now, we are breaking that contract and that's not ethical–no matter how much the child involved wants to know." This is one point of view that keeps names and identifying information securely locked in the social workers files. And you really must agree, this is a good point.

But this isn't without concern on the part of some social workers. "Now, we [in Nova Scotia] try to get a letter from the birth mother and from the adopting parents authorizing us to reveal the name to the child, should that child ask for it in the future. We don't give the identifying information at birth but we get a consent to release the information if asked by the child. That way, we can actively search in later years, if the child wants us to. We might not do that. The social worker would have to assess the situation and do the best thing for that time but we will have more options than we have now." The information would still be released at the discretion of the social worker and would not automatically be given to you. But, if your birth mother did give that kind of permission when you were born, the social worker may be able to help you when you search. "Adoptive parents and birth mothers could write in and change their consent to this information being released and we would have to respect that."

So, in spite of the very caring attitude that I felt from many social workers, the information they hold about searching adults who were adopted is controlled, by the law of the state or province, and they will not release it. In many cases, the laws cause a moral dilemma for the social worker. One worker from the Yukon Territory thought that the birth information belonged to the child, not to the welfare department, but she could not release the information to the child because the law of the Yukon would not allow her to.

The Yukon has a passive registry that holds the birth mother's name, if she submits it, and the child's information, if he submits it. With mutual consent, the social worker can bring about a re-union. But the worker, in spite of her personal feeling that the child has the right to the information, must hold that information secret until both parties agree to share it. A birth mother could write in now and give the social welfare department permission to release information to her child. If birth mothers were more aware of the problems their children are having trying to get information, perhaps more would write their permission.

The Northwest Territories of Canada is a land of vast tundra and awesome skies and a society that reflects space and freedom. It has a unique and practical adoption system.

I interviewed a worker in the Department of Social Services in Yellowknife, N.W.T. I asked her if children had difficulties in getting information about their birth parents. "Not really," she said. "We have a big area but we don't have a lot of people up here and everyone either knows everybody or they can get to know them. Kids can find their parents if they want to. I've worked here for nineteen years, and in this department for five and a half, and it's only in the last year or so that I've been getting inquiries about birth information. I don't get many inquiries from teenagers who are searching but if I do, I help them."

Me: "You help them search? Even if they are under nineteen?"

"Oh yes–if they have the permission of their adoptive parents. We don't have any legislation or any policies up here to prevent me from helping them. And it's really . . ." she hesitated, "it's really no big deal–no big secret. What's the matter down there? Do you have some kind of prejudice against adoption?"

She sounded so easy-going and reasonable that I wondered for a moment if we crazy southerners weren't making a big problem out of a simple matter.

Me: "Tell me about adoption in the Northwest."

"We have three different kinds of adoption. We have the department adoption which requires a medical, a waiting period, home studies and then all that paperwork after placement. We have very few children that come into our care that way, so we don't have many adoptions processed. Then we have private adoptions. Most adoptions are done that way. Usually a child is given to a family by a mother who lives in the same community. The department worker does a home study and after six months, the adoptive parents make arrangements with a lawyer to process the adoption legally. "

The third way is the native-custom adoption which is prearranged with the mother. There is no six-month probationary period. The adoption goes through when the baby is placed in the home. Three documents are signed and the child becomes a child of that family by order. This is done sometimes when families exchange children, that is, a family with four girls and a family with four boys might exchange a child. While this is often workable, young mothers are sometimes pressured into giving up their child to a family they don't really approve of–like a pensioner couple. But it's fast and convenient and doesn't cost any lawyer's fees and it usually works out all right.

I asked her about the teenagers need to search for their birth parents. "The only problems of identity that seem to come up are with the children who have been sent south. We didn't send many children south but those who went sometimes come back to look at their old home. We try to keep all our children in the Territories."

Me: "Do you have a policy of placing a child only with a family of his own race?"

"Well, now we don't have a real problem there, either. The department has so few children to place that we try to get the best home for the child and that includes looking at his race. Most of the private adoptions involve relatives or people in the same community, so it's approved of by the community, more or less. The adopting parents approach the mother and ask her for the child. If she likes the home, she'll put her baby there. It seems to work out pretty well."

I was impressed with the community solution to finding good homes for children–not a lot of official guidance, very little bureaucratic interference–just a community acceptance of some parents' need for children and some children's need for families.

"And because everyone knows who had the baby, it isn't hard for the child to find out his natural parents if he wants to. I helped a sixteen-year-old girl last week find her natural mother. Her adoptive mother thought it would be a good idea so she asked me to do it."

Me: "How long did it take you?"

"Twenty-four hours."

It seemed ideal. I tried to imagine the social situation in New York State or Ontario if those governments implemented the adoption system of the Northwest Territories. Life seemed a good deal simpler north of the sixtieth parallel.

Social workers in Ontario pick their way delicately through

the changing laws on adoption. A law prohibiting even an adopted adult from searching for any kind of information and prohibiting social workers from releasing any information, of any kind, to adopting parents or the child was passed in Ontario in 1985. However, the section concerning adoption information was not proclaimed, pending a study. The study recommended that adoption records be open.

I asked a social worker in Ontario how they dealt with the situation.

She said, "The laws that govern our lives change all the time and the problem of betraying a trust of eighteen years ago is less than the problem of maintaining secrecy and creating two categories of people in Canada–one that knows its beginnings and one that doesn't. Laws change all the time and no one can be expected to live under old laws. We have done a few small searches because we felt that the need to search was greater than the need to keep faith with the birth mother and we got permission from the deputy minister to do the search. In one case, a young man had leukemia and he needed a bone marrow transplant from a relative. We searched and found his birth mother. We've done that sort of thing a few times. But, for most people, we have to wait for the laws to change."

Me: "Do you feel that the birth information belongs to the agency or to the child?"

"I feel that anything written down in our agency belongs to the agency. But I sympathize with the child's need to know and, in fact, we very often recommend that an adopted adult search through the Children's Aid Society, if they were placed from there, or through the private agency that may have placed them, because those private agencies have more flexibility to give information than we do. They are semi-autonomous and, while they have to operate under the laws of Child Welfare, they are able to adjust and bend better than we can. Some private agencies give out much information and some don't."

In many cases, there seems to be the attitude that the social worker must protect society from itself; that all parties to the adoption, the child, the birth mother, the birth father, the adopting parents, must be organized and regulated by a social worker; that the parties involved could never reach a good decision without the professional advice of the adoption agency and its workers. In contrast, the attitude in the Northwest Territories seems to be that, if left alone with a minimum of interference, communities muddle through to a reasonably happy solution.

There is some indication that a trend is developing (Alberta's *Adoption Options*) where the birth mother and the adopting parents meet to discuss the baby's future, decide on how much contact they will have and exchange information *before* they approach the social worker.

In many provinces and states it is the policy of the welfare agencies that a child born in one city must be placed in another. If we changed that policy to approach that of the Northwest Territories we might place a child in the community or city in which he was born. This would encourage more open adoption, patterned after the welfare policies of many Native Indian communities, and perhaps, a more relaxed, reasonable attitude to the child's beginnings.

EPILOGUE

I met over forty of you while researching this book. Many people who heard I was writing a book about adoption called to talk to me: a birth father wanted to know if I had talked to his daughter; birth mothers wanted me to tell their children how they felt; foster children called; adoptive parents called; adults who had been adopted called; more teenagers called than I could possibly find the time to see. Everyone had a particular interest in some aspect of adoption.

I asked all teenagers the same questions, a list of twenty-nine, that covered many topics. Sometimes you stayed within range of the questions; sometimes the questions were only a stimulus for long conversations about your present life, your past, your expectations.

I couldn't predict how you would answer all the questions I asked but, after about ten interviews, I was quite sure how you would answer some of the questions. You had many feelings and ideas that you had arrived at independently, but held in common.

You wanted to know your original name, why you were given up for adoption, and your general social and medical history. You wanted either to meet your birth mother or to see her. You wanted to be in control of any meeting with birth parents. You didn't want substitute parents, just knowledge of your beginnings.

You usually didn't know how to search for information. You didn't know where to start or whom to call. You had vague ideas that somewhere there would be an accurate record of your birth and original name: in some hospital, in some welfare office, in some lawyer's office. Most of you thought social welfare offices held your personal background information in secret and resented the system that refused to give you this information. You didn't see yourselves as having the power to make changes in the system. You looked on your need to know about your birth as a personal and private need and, generally, hadn't thought much about the fact that there are many teenagers with similar needs.

You did not think that "being adopted" in any way restricted your social opportunities; you didn't feel any social prejudice against adoption. You didn't see the fact that you were adopted would in any way restrict your employment, social opportunities or family life. You would adopt children yourselves.

In other ways, you were all different. You had different needs for information, different emotional responses to families, to friends. You had different degrees of independence, ambition, and ability. Some had few concerns about the process of adoption, some had many. Some poured out their feelings about the problems society caused them; others couldn't see what the fuss was all about.

You were interesting, informative and eager to share your ideas. You were especially eager to share with other teenagers who had thought your thoughts, lived with your worries and shared your feelings.

You are part of the changing attitudes toward adoption. The attitudes that will affect the next generation are being changed by what you do today. The first step in making changes is to understand yourself, to know what you think and why. Perhaps this book will help you take that first step, help you begin to know how you feel, what you want, what you need.

APPENDIX I

WHERE YOU CAN GET HELP

The best source of information I have found for articles and lists of books is:

Adoption Resource Center, Rm 28 10950 159 St., Edmonton, Alberta, Canada T5P 3C1

If you write to this address you will be sent a list from which you can choose books and papers under specific headings such as: Searching, Parenting, Interracial Adoption, Adoptive Parenting, Advocacy, International Adoption, Birth Parents and Open Adoption. There are other addresses found in newspapers, telephone books and lists in libraries that provide information and help. Your local library is a good place to start. Some addresses are listed below.

Canadian Adoption Reunion Register, 686 Hampshire Rd., Victoria, B.C., Canada, V8S 4S2

International Soundex Reunion Register, Mrs. Emma May Vilardi, Box 2312, Carson City, Nevada, U.S.A. 89701

Parent Finders Groups Listed in local phone books and city directories

Joan Vanstone, 1408 West 45th, Vancouver, B.C., Canada V6M 2H1

Parent Finders Inc., Box 272, Willowdale, Stn. A, ON, Canada, M2N 5T1

People Finders, 528 S. Batavia Ave., Ste. 2A, Batavia, IL, 60510 (312) 879-6853

Chris Spurr, 1602 Cole, Birmingham, MI, 48008

Marie Pauline Lamarach, Box 52, Old Westbury, Long Island, NY, 11568

OTHER GROUPS

Canadian Adoptee's Reform Association, #202-4381 Fraser St., Vancouver, B.C., Canada V5V 2G4

Triad, Box 5114 Stn. A, Calgary, Alberta, Canada T2H 1X1

American Adoption Congress, Sophie Elvert, Box 44040, L'Enfant Plaza Stn., Washington D.C., U.S.A. 20026-0040

Triadoption Library, Mary Jo Rillera, 7571 Westminster Ave., Westminster, California, U.S.A. 92683

Spark, Box 197, Cabot, VT, 05647

Jigsaw Victoria, Box 5260 BB, Melbourne, Victoria 3001, Australia

Jigsaw Inc., Josie Hendry, Box 9228, Newmarket, Auckland, New Zealand

Search Triad, Inc., P. O. Box 1432, Litchfield, AZ, 86001 (602) 935-1405

Adoptees Research Association, P.O Box 304, Montrose, CA, 91020

Triad, Inc., P. O. Box 4778, Columbia, S.C., 29407

TRIAD Research, 300 Golden West, Shafter, CA, 93263

Triadoption Library, P. O. Box 638, Westminster, CA, 92684

Organized Adp'n. Search Info. Serv. (OASIS), (Headquarters), P. O. Box 53-0761, Miami Shores, FL, 33153, (305) 945-2758

Adoptees Search Network, 3317 Spring Creek Dr., Conyers, GA, 30208

Reunion Registry of Indiana, P. O. Box 361, South Bend, IN, 46624

Iowa Reference & Reunion Library, P. O. Box 9191, Cedar Rapids, IA, 52409

Adoption Triad Network, Inc., P. O. Box 3932, Lafayette, LA, 70502, (318) 235-7983

Minnesota Reunion Registry, 23247 Lofton Ct. No., Scandia, MN, 55073

Midwest Adoption Triad, P. O. Box 37262, Omaha, NE, 68137

Birthdates Registry, 117 Nelson Ave., Jersey City, NJ, 07840
Nat'l Adoptive Search Registry (NASR), P. O. Box 2051, Great Nack, NY, 11022
Adoptees Liberty Movement Assn. (ALMA), (Headquarters), P. O. Box 154, Wash. Bridge Stn., New York City, NY, 10033, (212) 581-1568
Washington Adoptees Rights Movement (WARM), 220 Kirkland Ave. 10, Kirland, WA, 98003

Starting to educate yourself about adoption, starting to search for your background through the many mistakes, discouragements and false starts that occur is something like beginning the first stitches of a Queen-sized afghan. You hold the crochet hook in your hand, see the tiny three or four stitches you've started, and wonder how you will ever have the patience and determination you need to work stitch after stitch after stitch for years until you produce the finished blanket. If you can envision yourself starting, ripping out the mistakes, starting again, adding small stitch by small stitch until you create an afghan, then you can envision yourself amassing small bits of information, pursuing wrong leads, starting again and slowly, painstakingly creating a picture of your own background.

The people in the organizations listed above know what that process takes in determination and perserverance. They can understand your need to do it and they can help.

APPENDIX II

QUESTIONNAIRE

Name or Number _____

Age (not birth date)_____Male_____Female_____

Mother's age_____Father's age_____

Siblings:

Age_____adopted also_____yes_____no_____

Age_____adopted also_____yes_____no_____

Age_____adopted also_____yes_____no_____

1. When were you told you were adopted?_____Always known_____

2. Why did your natural parents give you up for adoption?

_____Don't know_____

Why do you think they did?_____

At what age were you placed for adoption?_____

3. Why did your present parents adopt you?

_____

Why do you think they did?_____

_____

4. Do you get along with your parents?

       Most of the time_____Hardly ever_____

5. How do you rate your parents 1-10?_____

6. Will your parents help you with your future plans?_____

7. What class do you put yourself in?

       Head_____Jock_____Preppie_____Achiever_____

       Loser_____Average_____Other_____

8. What is your ambition?_____

9. Have you ever heard anything bad about adoption?_____

       What?_____

10. Have you ever heard anything good about adoption?_____

       What?_____

11. Do your relatives treat you differently from your brothers and sisters because you are adopted?_____

       How?_____

       Does it hurt?_____

12. Do your friends and neighbors think you don't belong in your family because you are adopted?_____

13. Do your brothers and sisters treat you differently because you are adopted?_____

       Does it hurt?_____

14. How much do you think environment (family, friends, community) affects your life (in percentage)_____

15. How much do you think heredity (your physical make up, your genes, the tendencies you were born with) affects your life. (in percentage)_____

16. What do you know about your natural parents

       Social history_____

       Medical history_____

       Names known_____ unknown_____

17. What do you want to know about your natural parents?

       _____

18. What difference would knowing about your natural parents make to you?

19. How does "being adopted" affect your life?

Postively_____Negatively_____or does it_____

20. How does "being adopted" affect your future?

Postively_____Negatively_____or does it_____

21. What rights can you expect to get from your adoptive parents? What do you think they owe you?_____

What are your responsibilities to them?_____

22. What rights can you expect to get from your natural parent? What do they owe you?_____

What are your responsibilities to them?_____

23. Is your birth and the details of your birth important to you, such as where you were born, how much you weighed?

24. Do you want to find your natural mother? yes_____no_____maybe_____

your natural father? yes_____no_____maybe_____

Why?_____

25. Do you know how you could find them?_____

What have you tried?_____

26. How would you fit your natural parents in your life if they came knocking on your door today?_____

How would you fit them into your future?_____

27. Today, in society we have many different kinds of relationships: common-law marriages, short-term coupling, long-term commitment. Families are composed of natural children, step-children, adopted children.

How do you see the family of the future?_____

_____

How do you see your own "married" life?_____

_____

28. Would you adopt children yourself?_____

    Why?_____

    Why not?_____

29. What music do you like?

    Punk_____Soft Rock_____Hard Rock_____

    New Wave_____Jazz_____Folk_____

    Country_____Classical_____Reggae_____

BIBLIOGRAPHY

Ames, Elinor Phd. "Psychological studies on adoption." British Columbia Medical Journal Vol. 26, Number 3, March 1984

Burgess, Linda Canon. *The art of adoption.* New York: W.W.Norton and Co., 1981

Bunin, Sherry. *Is that your sister.* New York: Patheon, 1976

DuPrau, Jeanne. *Adoption: the facts, feelings and issues of a double heritage.* New York: Messner, 1981

Fisher, Florence. *The search for Anna Fisher.* New York: Fawcett Books, 1973

Kaushin, Alfred. *Adopting older Children.* Columbia University Press, 1970

Kirk, H. David. *Shared Fate.* London: Collier-Macmillian, 1964 (revised Brentwood Bay: Ben-Simon Publications, 1984)

Kowenty, Jill. *How it Feels to be Adopted.* New York: Alfred A. Knopf, 1982

Joyce, A. *Adopting Across Racial Boundaries.* Garden City, New York: Anchor Press, 1978

Lawrence, Margaret McDonald. "Inside, looking out of adoption." Paper presented to the 84th annual convention of the American Psychological Association Division 29, in Washington D.C., Sept. 4, 1976

Lapsley, Susan. Illustrator, Michael Charlton. *I am adopted.* Bodley Head, 1983

Livingstone, Carole. *Why was I adopted.* North American Council on Adoptable Children

Lifton, Betty Jean. *Twice Born: Memoirs of an Adopted Daughter.* New York: Penquin Books, 1977

---------. *Lost and Found: The Adoption Experience.* New York: Dial Press, 1983

Lund, Doris. *Patchwork Clan. How the Sweeney family grew.* New York: Little Brown and Co. 1982

Marcus, Claire. *Adopted? a Canadian guide for adopted adults in search of their origins.* Vancouver: International Self-Counsel Press, 1979

---------. *Who is my mother? birth parents, adoptive parents and adoptees talk about living with adoption and the search for lost family.* Toronto: Macmillan of Canada, 1981

McTaggart, Lynne. *The Baby Brokers.* New York: Dial Press, 1980

Nickman, Steven. *The Adoption Experience.* New York: J. Messner, 1985

Powledge, Fred. *So You're Adopted.* New York: Scribner, 1982

Pursell, Margaret Sanford. Photographer Maria S. Forrai. *A look at adoption.* Lerner Publications (U.S.A.), Dent and Sons (Canada) 1978

Redmond, Wendie. *Once Removed from Inside the Adoption Triangle.* Toronto: McGraw-Hill Ryerson, 1982

Revised Statutes of Alberta 1986, ch 8

Revised Statutes of Manitoba 1974, ch 30

Revised Statutes of New Brunswick, 1973, ch A-3

Revised Statutes of Nova Scotia 1967, ch 2

Revised Statutes of Ontario 1980, ch 66

Revised Statutes of Quebec 1977, ch A-7

Revised Statutes of Prince Edward Island 1974, ch A-1

Revised Statutes of Saskcatchewan 1978, ch F-7

Rosenbury, Maxine B. *Being Adopted.* New York: Lothrop Lee and Shepard, 1984

Rubin, Lillina B. *Intimate Strangers.* New York: Harper Calophon Books, 1983

Sabol, Harriet Longsam. Photography Patricia Agre. *We don't look like Mom and Dad.* New York: Coward MacCann, 1984

Stein, Sara Bonnett. Photography Erika Stone. *The Adopted One: an open family book for parents and children together.* New York: Walden and Co., 1979

Storr, Catherine. *Vicky.* Faber and Faber, 1981

Sweeney, John. Sweeney releases Garber report on adoption disclosure. News Release. November 29, 1985

Tonkin, Roger,M.D. "Adolescents and adoption." British Columbia Medical Journal Vol. 26, No. 3, March 1984

--------- "The physician and the adolescent adoptee. British Columbia Medical Journal Vol. 26, No. 3, March 1984"

Triseliotes, John. *In Search of Origins; the experiences of adopted people.* London: Rutledge and Kegan Parl, 1973